The Australian Women's
Weekly
cookbooks

I simply couldn't do this job if I didn't love food and cooking. But as we test and taste all day in the Test Kitchen, I sometimes feel that my resolve to eat less fat is being sorely tried. That's why *Low-Fat Feasts* is such a welcome addition to the collection. Not only can I cook special meals for my family and friends, I can do so knowing that even if we eat three courses, the total fat count will still be under 30g. That's worth celebrating in itself. Even the testing and tasting was guilt-free for this one!

Pamela Clark

Food Editor

contents

celebrate

Every recipe in *Low-Fat Feasts* has been carefully compiled to allow you to create delicious meals – starter, main course and dessert – that contain no more than 30g fat in total. We've even included some sweet treats to serve with coffee and, if you don't tell them, your guests will never know they're eating low-fat food.

We've all encountered the problem at some stage – we've made the decision to adopt a healthier lifestyle, reduced our fat intake, even begun to see positive results, when the whole plan is sabotaged by a weekend's festivities.

So what's the answer? There is no doubt that a diet lower in fat, and specifically, lower in saturated fat, is important for maintaining good health, particularly for those people prone to heart disease and diabetes. But does this mean that there can be no more "cakes and ale", that

steamed fish and vegies are on the menu forever? Well, the good news is that of course it needn't mean this and, while steamed fish and fresh vegetables do make a delicious low-fat meal, when it comes to special occasions and celebrations, there is no reason to miss out on any of the good things.

We've created all the meals in *Low-Fat Feasts* to prove that a healthier diet does not need to involve deprivation and "diet" food. Indeed, as you look through the recipes in the book, you'll be delighted by the variety and range of

flavours. Can this really be low-fat food? It most certainly is.

Life is full of reasons for celebrating and what would any celebration be without food and the company of friends? Sharing a meal with friends is one of the most fundamental pleasures and it becomes even more pleasurable when you know the food itself is actually good for you.

So go ahead and celebrate. This is a book to help you enjoy all those good things in life without compromising your decision to choose the low-fat option.

pea flapjacks with smoked trout

preparation time 30 minutes • cooking time 15 minutes

400g whole smoked trout
1/2 cup (75g) plain flour
1/2 cup (75g) self-raising flour
1/4 teaspoon bicarbonate of soda
2/3 cup (160ml) buttermilk
1/3 cup (80ml) skim milk
1/2 cup (60g) frozen peas,
    thawed, drained
1 tablespoon finely chopped
    fresh flat-leaf parsley
2 tablespoons finely chopped
    fresh chives
1 egg white
1/4 cup (60g) low-fat sour cream

PICKLED CUCUMBER
2 lebanese cucumbers (260g)
1 small red capsicum (150g),
    chopped finely
1/4 cup (60ml) water
1/4 cup (55g) sugar
1/2 cup (125ml) white vinegar

1. Remove any skin and bones from fish; break into large pieces.
2. Sift flours and soda into large bowl; gradually whisk in combined buttermilk, skim milk, peas, parsley and half of the chives.
3. Beat egg white in small bowl with rotary or electric mixer until soft peaks form; fold egg white into batter. Pour 1/3 cup (60ml) of the batter for each flapjack in large heated oiled non-stick frying pan; cook, in batches, until browned lightly both sides.
4. Combine sour cream and remaining chives in small bowl. Serve warm flapjacks topped with fish, pickled cucumber and sour cream mixture.

pickled cucumber Using vegetable peeler, slice cucumbers into ribbons. Combine cucumber in medium bowl with capsicum. Combine the water and sugar in small saucepan; stir over low heat until sugar dissolves. Bring to a boil; reduce heat. Simmer, uncovered, about 5 minutes or until thickened slightly. Add vinegar to sugar syrup; pour hot syrup over cucumber mixture. Cover; refrigerate until cool.

serves 6

per serving 4.2g fat; 925kJ

tip Pickled cucumber can be made a day ahead and refrigerated, covered.

serving suggestion Smoked salmon can be used as an alternative to the trout.

Smoked trout are available from specialty food shops and fishmongers.

starters

chicken wonton soup

preparation time 20 minutes (plus refrigeration time) • cooking time 2 hours 10 minutes

The wontons in this southern Chinese speciality make the soup short as distinct from long soup which contains noodles.

2kg chicken bones
2 medium brown onions (300g),
    chopped coarsely
2 trimmed sticks celery (150g),
    chopped coarsely
2 medium carrots (240g),
    chopped coarsely
3 bay leaves
2 teaspoons black peppercorns
5 litres (20 cups) water
2 tablespoons dark soy sauce
1 clove garlic, crushed
1 teaspoon grated fresh ginger
500g baby bok choy, chopped coarsely
2 green onions, sliced thinly

CHICKEN WONTONS
300g chicken mince
1 tablespoon dark soy sauce
1 clove garlic, crushed
1 teaspoon sesame oil
4 green onions, chopped finely
40 wonton wrappers

1. Combine bones, brown onion, celery, carrot, bay leaves, peppercorns and the water in large saucepan; bring to a boil. Reduce heat; simmer, uncovered, 2 hours, skimming occasionally.
2. Strain stock through muslin-lined strainer into large bowl; discard bones and other solids. Cover stock; refrigerate 3 hours or overnight.
3. Remove and discard fat from surface of stock. Return stock to large saucepan with sauce, garlic and ginger. Bring to a boil; reduce heat. Add chicken wontons; simmer, uncovered, about 5 minutes or until wontons float to surface.
4. Just before serving soup, stir in remaining ingredients.
chicken wontons Combine chicken, sauce, garlic, oil and onion in medium bowl. Brush edge of each wonton wrapper with water. Place rounded teaspoon of chicken mixture in centre of wrapper; pinch edges together to seal. Repeat with remaining wrappers and chicken mixture.

serves 8

per serving 5.8g fat; 720kJ

tip Stock and wontons can be made in advance and frozen, separately.

serving suggestion Accompany with a mixture of finely chopped red thai chillies, coriander and mint.

roasted pumpkin, sesame and rocket salad

preparation time 15 minutes • cooking time 25 minutes

You will need a piece of pumpkin weighing approximately 750g for this recipe; we used butternut, but you can use whatever pumpkin variety you like.

600g trimmed pumpkin
cooking-oil spray
1 tablespoon honey
1 tablespoon sesame seeds
500g asparagus, halved
150g baby rocket leaves
1 small red onion (100g), sliced thinly
1 tablespoon sesame oil
1 tablespoon cider vinegar
1 teaspoon honey, extra

1. Preheat oven to very hot.
2. Cut pumpkin into 1.5cm wide strips.
3. Place pumpkin, in single layer, in baking dish lined with baking paper; spray lightly with cooking-oil spray. Roast, uncovered, in very hot oven about 20 minutes or until pumpkin is just tender. Drizzle with honey; sprinkle with seeds. Roast 5 minutes, uncovered, or until seeds are browned lightly.
4. Meanwhile, boil, steam or microwave asparagus until just tender; drain. Rinse under cold water; drain.
5. Combine pumpkin, asparagus, rocket and onion in large bowl. Drizzle with combined remaining ingredients; toss salad gently .

serves 6

per serving 5.3g fat; 505kJ

tip Reserve any seeds or honey from pumpkin pan and add to dressing.

serving suggestion Serve with warmed or toasted pide.

lamb fillo triangles

preparation time 30 minutes • cooking time 20 minutes

From the Greek word meaning leaf, fillo means paper-thin sheets of dough, which give the crunch and pleasure of pastry without the kilojoules.

2 cloves garlic, crushed

1 teaspoon ground cumin

1 teaspoon ground coriander

1/4 teaspoon ground cinnamon

1 tablespoon pine nuts

250g lean lamb mince

2 tablespoons sultanas

1 tablespoon coarsely chopped
   fresh coriander

1 tablespoon coarsely chopped
   fresh mint

16 sheets fillo pastry

cooking-oil spray

1 1/2 cups (420g) low-fat yogurt

1/2 cup finely shredded fresh mint

1. Cook garlic, spices and pine nuts in medium heated dry non-stick frying pan about 1 minute or until fragrant. Add lamb; cook, stirring, until lamb is browned and cooked through. Add sultanas, coriander and chopped mint; stir until just combined. Cool 5 minutes.

2. Preheat oven to moderately hot.

3. Brush one sheet of the fillo lightly with water; layer with second sheet of fillo. Cut lengthways into thirds. Place 1 tablespoon of the mixture at bottom of one narrow edge of fillo pieces, leaving a 1cm border. Fold opposite corner of fillo diagonally across the filling to form a triangle; continue folding to end of fillo piece, retaining triangle shape. Place on lightly oiled oven trays, seam-side down; repeat with remaining ingredients until 24 triangles are made.

4. Spray triangles lightly with cooking-oil spray; bake, uncovered, in moderately hot oven about 10 minutes or until browned lightly.

5. Serve fillo triangles with combined yogurt and shredded mint.

serves 8

per serving 5.8g fat; 805kJ

tip Triangles can be prepared in advance and frozen, covered. No need to thaw before baking; just place on oven trays and cook until browned.

serving suggestion To make this a more substantial meal, serve it with a Greek salad made with low-fat fetta cheese.

baked ricotta with roasted capsicum salad

preparation time 15 minutes • cooking time 30 minutes (plus standing time)

200g low-fat ricotta cheese
2 tablespoons finely grated
   parmesan cheese
1 egg, beaten lightly
1 teaspoon coarsely chopped
   fresh sage
3 fresh bay leaves, chopped coarsely
2 medium red capsicums (400g)
2 medium yellow capsicums (400g)
250g mesclun
1/4 cup (60ml) balsamic vinegar
1 tablespoon olive oil
1 tablespoon honey

1. Preheat oven to moderately slow.
2. Oil eight holes of a 12-hole
1/3-cup (80ml) non-stick muffin pan.
Combine cheeses and egg in small bowl.
Divide ricotta mixture among prepared
holes; sprinkle with combined herbs.
3. Place muffin pan in large baking
dish; add enough boiling water to come
halfway up side of pan. Bake ricotta,
uncovered, in moderately slow oven
about 30 minutes or until set. Stand
10 minutes before turning ricottas out.
4. Meanwhile, quarter capsicums;
remove and discard seeds and
membranes. Roast under grill or in very
hot oven, skin-side up, until skin blisters
and blackens. Cover capsicum pieces
with plastic or paper 5 minutes. Peel
away skin; slice capsicum thickly.
5. Place capsicum and mesclun in large
bowl with combined remaining
ingredients. Divide salad among serving
plates; top each with a baked ricotta.

serves 8

per serving 5.8g fat; 430kJ

tip Dried bay leaves and 1/4 teaspoon
crumbled dried sage can be substituted
for the fresh varieties.

serving suggestion Serve as an
appetiser to a pasta main course.

*The word ricotta means re-cooked, a reference to the fact that this
moist fresh cheese is made from the leftover whey after stretched-curd
cheeses such as mozzarella or provolone are produced.*

mussel chowder

preparation time 20 minute • cooking time 30 minutes

The name chowder came from the French word, chaudière, for the cauldron in which fishermen made their stews fresh from the sea. The Americans adopted this thick chunky soup as their own – New England chowders are made with milk or cream, while in Manhattan they use tomatoes for the base.

1kg mussels
1 teaspoon olive oil
1 small leek (200g), sliced thinly
2 large potatoes (600g), chopped finely
2 trimmed sticks celery (150g), chopped finely
1/2 cup (125ml) dry white wine
2 cups (500ml) fish stock
2 cups (500ml) water
30g butter
2 tablespoons plain flour
1 cup (250ml) skim milk
1 tablespoon finely chopped fresh flat-leaf parsley
1 tablespoon finely chopped fresh chives

1. Scrub mussels under cold running water; remove beards.
2. Heat oil in large saucepan; cook leek, potato and celery, stirring, until leek softens. Add wine; boil, uncovered, until wine reduces by half. Add stock and the water; bring to a boil. Reduce heat; simmer, uncovered, about 20 minutes or until potato is tender.
3. Meanwhile, melt butter in small saucepan; cook flour, stirring, 1 minute. Add milk; bring to a boil. Reduce heat; simmer, stirring, until sauce thickens.
4. Blend or process half of the chowder mixture, in batches, until smooth. Return to pan with remaining chowder; stir in sauce.
5. Add mussels to pan; bring to a boil. Reduce heat; simmer chowder, covered, about 5 minutes or until all mussels open (discard any that do not). Serve in bowls; sprinkle with herbs.

serves 6

per serving 6.0g; 776kJ

serving suggestion Serve with a warm baguette, sliced, for dunking in the soup.

After pulling the seaweed threads or beards away from mussels, scrub shells with a stiff brush under cold water.

smoked chicken salad

preparation time 15 minutes

Smoked chicken has already been cooked during the curing process, making this a simple salad to put together at short notice. You can keep a smoked chicken in your freezer; just thaw before slicing.

400g smoked chicken breast
200g baby spinach leaves
1 medium yellow capsicum (200g),
　sliced thinly
1 medium red onion (170g),
　sliced thinly
1 cup firmly packed fresh purple
　basil leaves
2 teaspoons finely grated lime rind
1/4 cup (60ml) lime juice
2 tablespoons coarsely chopped
　fresh coriander
2 red thai chillies, seeded,
　chopped finely
2 teaspoons peanut oil
1 teaspoon sugar

1. Remove and discard any skin from chicken; slice chicken thinly.
2. Combine chicken, spinach, capsicum, onion and basil in large bowl.
3. Combine remaining ingredients in screw-top jar; shake well.
4. Pour dressing over salad; toss gently to combine.

serves 8

per serving 3.9g fat; 363kJ

serving suggestion Serve with corn bread or flour tortillas.

gazpacho

preparation time 10 minutes (plus standing time) • cooking time 10 minutes

2 medium red capsicums (400g)
1 litre (4 cups) vegetable juice
2 tablespoons red wine vinegar
1/2 teaspoon Tabasco sauce
1 clove garlic, quartered
3 trimmed sticks celery (225g),
    chopped finely
1 medium red onion (170g),
    chopped finely
5 medium tomatoes (950g),
    chopped finely
2 telegraph cucumbers (800g), peeled,
    seeded, chopped finely

1. Quarter capsicums; remove and discard seeds and membranes. Roast under grill or in very hot oven, skin-side up, until skin blisters and blackens. Cover capsicum pieces with plastic or paper 5 minutes. Peel away and discard skin; chop coarsely.
2. Blend or process capsicum with juice, vinegar, sauce, garlic and half of the celery, onion, tomato and cucumber until smooth; transfer mixture to large bowl. Cover; refrigerate about 1 hour or until cold. Refrigerate remaining half of the chopped vegetables.
3. Divide gazpacho among serving dishes; top each with reserved chopped vegetables just before serving.

serves 8

per serving 0.4g fat; 268kJ

tip Traditional accompaniments for this soup include croutons and diced hard-boiled egg.

serving suggestion Serve in glass tumblers with a celery swizzle stick.

The cooks of Andalucia devised this refreshing chilled soup possibly as an antidote to the passions aroused by those other contributions to Spanish culture – flamenco and bullfighting. Often called a pureed salad, gazpacho sometimes has stale breadcrumbs blended in with the vegetables to make it a heartier meal.

Parmesan is best bought in a block and grated when required, as pre-grated parmesan quickly loses its flavour.

low-fat caesar salad

preparation time 10 minutes • cooking time 15 minutes

The original caesar salad is said to have been created in the 1920s by an Italian chef, Caesar Cardini, at his restaurant in Tijuana, Mexico.

4 slices white bread
4 slices prosciutto (40g)
1/4 cup (70g) low-fat yogurt
1/4 cup (75g) low-fat mayonnaise
2 cloves garlic, quartered
5 anchovy fillets, drained
1/2 teaspoon worcestershire sauce
1/2 teaspoon dijon mustard
11/2 tablespoons lemon juice
4 baby cos lettuces
1/4 cup (20g) finely grated
  parmesan cheese

1. Preheat oven to moderate.
2. Remove crusts from bread; cut bread into 1cm cubes. Place on oven tray; bake, uncovered, in moderate oven about 5 minutes or until croutons are just toasted lightly.
3. Meanwhile, fry prosciutto, uncovered, stirring, in medium heated dry non-stick frying pan until browned and crisp; chop coarsely.
4. Blend or process yogurt, mayonnaise, garlic, anchovy, sauce, mustard and juice until almost smooth.
5. Combine croutons, prosciutto, yogurt mixture, lettuce leaves and cheese; toss gently to combine.

serves 8

per serving 3.6g fat; 350kJ

watercress salad

preparation time 25 minutes • cooking time 2 minutes

We used corella pears for this recipe. You will need a bunch of watercress weighing about 350g in total to yield the leaves required for this salad.

3 small pears (540g), sliced thinly
1 teaspoon finely grated orange rind
½ cup (125ml) orange juice
300g snow peas, trimmed
100g watercress leaves

CHEESE BALLS

150g low-fat ricotta cheese
100g low-fat fetta cheese
¼ cup (30g) finely grated
   cheddar cheese
1 tablespoon finely chopped
   fresh flat-leaf parsley
1 tablespoon finely chopped
   fresh chives
2 teaspoons finely chopped
   fresh thyme
1 teaspoon curry powder
1 teaspoon sweet paprika

1. Combine pear, rind and juice in large bowl. Cover; refrigerate 15 minutes.
2. Meanwhile, boil, steam or microwave snow peas until just tender; drain. Rinse under cold water; drain.
3. Gently toss pear mixture, snow peas and watercress in large bowl. Serve topped with cheese balls.

cheese balls Combine cheeses, parsley, chives and thyme in small bowl. Roll level teaspoons of mixture into balls. Combine curry powder and paprika in small bowl; gently toss half of the cheese balls in curry mixture until coated.

serves 6

per serving 6.2g fat; 666kJ

serving suggestion Serve as an appetiser before grilled or barbecued steak or lamb.

oven-baked spring rolls

preparation time 30 minutes • cooking time 20 minutes

Named because they are usually served on the first day of the Chinese New Year (early in the Northern Hemisphere's spring), spring rolls are a perennially popular appetiser. Here, they're baked instead of deep-fried, reducing the kilojoule count dramatically. You need about half a small chinese cabbage to make this recipe.

4 dried shiitake mushrooms
5 green onions, sliced thinly
1 clove garlic, crushed
1 teaspoon grated fresh ginger
1 medium red capsicum (200g), sliced thinly
2 cups (160g) finely shredded chinese cabbage
1/3 cup (65g) canned bamboo shoots, drained, sliced thinly
1 tablespoon light soy sauce
1 tablespoon sweet chilli sauce
1/2 teaspoon fish sauce
1/4 cup loosely packed, finely chopped fresh coriander
1 cup (80g) bean sprouts
15 sheets fillo pastry
cooking-oil spray

CHILLI SOY DIPPING SAUCE

1/4 cup (60ml) light soy sauce
1/4 cup (60ml) sweet chilli sauce
2 tablespoons lime juice
1 teaspoon sugar
1 tablespoon finely chopped fresh coriander
1 red thai chilli, seeded, chopped finely

1. Place mushrooms in small heatproof bowl; cover with boiling water. Stand 20 minutes or until tender; drain. Discard stems; slice caps thinly.
2. Preheat oven to moderately hot.
3. Heat large lightly oiled non-stick frying pan; cook onion, garlic and ginger, stirring, until onion softens. Add mushrooms, capsicum, cabbage, bamboo shoots and combined sauces; cook, stirring, until cabbage just wilts. Remove from heat; stir in coriander and sprouts. Drain away excess liquid.
4. Cut fillo sheets in half. Spray one piece fillo with cooking-oil spray; fold in half crossways. Spray again with cooking-oil spray; turn fillo so folded edge is on your right and one short side faces you. Place 1 tablespoon of the vegetable mixture 2cm from bottom edge of fillo. Fold in sides; roll bottom to top to enclose filling. Repeat with remaining pieces fillo and filling.
5. Place rolls on oiled oven tray. Bake, uncovered, in moderately hot oven about 15 minutes or until rolls are browned lightly. Serve rolls with chilli soy dipping sauce.

chilli soy dipping sauce Combine ingredients in small bowl.

makes 30

per roll 1.8g fat; 173kJ

tip You can vary the vegetables in the filling to suit your personal taste.

serving suggestion Serve as an appetiser before a stir-fry or noodle main course.

Baking rather than deep-frying both reduces the fat count and keeps the filling from becoming soggy.

leek and asparagus risotto

preparation time 15 minutes • cooking time 45 minutes

Arborio is a small, wide-grained, pearly rice variety which is ideal for making risotto as it readily absorbs stock without becoming mushy.

1½ cups (375ml) dry white wine
1.5 litres (6 cups) chicken stock
2 teaspoons low-fat dairy-free spread
2 medium leeks (700g), sliced thinly
2 cloves garlic, crushed
3 cups (600g) arborio rice
500g asparagus, trimmed,
    chopped coarsely
⅓ cup (25g) finely grated
    parmesan cheese

1. Combine wine and stock in large saucepan; bring to a boil. Reduce heat; simmer, covered, to keep hot.
2. Meanwhile, heat dairy-free spread in large saucepan; cook leek and garlic, stirring, until leek softens. Add rice; stir to coat in leek mixture. Stir in 1 cup of the hot stock mixture; cook, stirring, over low heat until liquid is absorbed. Continue adding stock mixture, in 1-cup batches, stirring, until liquid is absorbed after each addition. Total cooking time should be about 30 minutes or until rice is just tender.
3. Add asparagus; cook, stirring, until asparagus is just tender. Just before serving, stir in cheese.

serves 8

per serving 2.9g fat; 1483kJ

serving suggestion Serve sprinkled with freshly ground black pepper and finely chopped fresh basil leaves.

Fresh sugar snap peas can be substituted for the asparagus, if preferred.

char-grilled polenta cakes

preparation time 15 minutes (plus refrigeration time) • cooking time 20 minutes

Polenta is made by grinding dried yellow or white corn (maize) kernels to a rough-textured meal.

cooking-oil spray
1 litre (4 cups) water
1 teaspoon salt
1 cup (170g) polenta
2 tablespoons seeded mustard
2 trimmed corn cobs (500g)
1 medium red capsicum (200g),
    chopped finely
1 medium red onion (170g),
    chopped finely
1 lebanese cucumber (130g),
    seeded, chopped finely
1/4 cup loosely packed, coarsely
    chopped fresh flat-leaf parsley
1 teaspoon finely grated lime rind
1/3 cup (80ml) lime juice
2 tablespoons olive oil
3 cloves garlic, crushed
1 tablespoon sweet chilli sauce

1. Lightly spray 23cm-square slab cake pan with cooking-oil spray. Bring the water and salt to a boil in large saucepan. Add polenta; cook, stirring, about 10 minutes or until polenta thickens. Add mustard; stir until combined. Spread polenta into slab pan. Cover; refrigerate about 30 minutes or until firm.
2. Meanwhile, boil, steam or microwave corn until just tender. Drain; cool. Using sharp knife, remove kernels from cob. Combine corn in medium bowl with remaining ingredients.
3. Turn polenta onto board; cut into eight rectangles. Heat large lightly oiled non-stick frying pan; cook polenta, in batches, until browned both sides. Serve polenta cakes with corn salsa.

serves 8

per serving 6.3g fat; 753kJ

tip You can reduce preparation and cooking times by substituting the fresh corn for a 420g can of corn kernels, drained.

serving suggestion Serve with a salad of rocket or mixed baby greens.

Fresh lasagne sheets, available loose by weight from good delis or in cryovac packages from supermarkets, take virtually no time at all to pre-cook.

pasta with fresh tomato sauce

preparation time 15 minutes • cooking time 5 minutes

This is a great short-order dish which can be prepared in about the time it takes to warm the bread and open the wine.

375g fresh lasagne sheets,
  sliced thickly
2 tablespoons extra virgin olive oil
6 medium tomatoes (1.2kg), peeled,
  seeded, chopped coarsely
1/4 cup loosely packed, coarsely
  chopped fresh basil
2 cloves garlic, crushed
2 teaspoons red wine vinegar
1 red thai chilli, seeded,
  chopped finely
80g low-fat fetta cheese, crumbled

1. Cook pasta in large saucepan of boiling water, uncovered, until just tender; drain. Sprinkle half of the oil over pasta; toss gently to combine.
2. Combine tomato, basil, garlic, remaining oil, vinegar and chilli in medium bowl.
3. Divide pasta among serving plates. Spoon tomato mixture over pasta; sprinkle with cheese.

serves 8

per serving 6.3g fat; 535kJ

tip To peel tomatoes, slice a cross in the bottom of tomato. Place tomatoes in large bowl of boiling water 1 minute; drain. Rinse under cold water; peel.

serving suggestion Serve with crusty bread and a green salad.

steamed sweet chilli prawn dumplings

preparation time 20 minutes • cooking time 5 minutes

Try serving these dumplings as finger food, presenting them in the bamboo steamer in which they were cooked, with drinks before you and your guests go to the table.

500g medium uncooked prawns
2 tablespoons sweet chilli sauce
2 green onions, sliced thinly
1 clove garlic, crushed
1 teaspoon grated fresh ginger
2 tablespoons coarsely chopped
　fresh coriander
1 teaspoon finely chopped fresh
　lemon grass
24 gow gee wrappers

1. Shell and devein prawns; chop finely.
2. Combine prawn, sauce, onion, garlic, ginger, coriander and lemon grass in medium bowl.
3. Place 1 heaped teaspoon of the prawn filling in centre of each gow gee wrapper; brush edges with water. Fold wrapper in half to enclose filling; pinch edges together to seal.
4. Place dumplings, in batches, in single layer in bamboo steamer. Cook, covered, over wok or large saucepan of simmering water about 5 minutes or until dumplings are cooked through.

serves 6

per serving 0.7g fat; 368kJ

tip Wonton wrappers can be used as an alternative to gow gee wrappers.

serving suggestion Serve drizzled with extra sweet chilli sauce and a small bowl of soy sauce for dipping.

roasted vegetable fillo tart

preparation time 20 minutes • cooking time 45 minutes

6 medium egg tomatoes
  (450g), quartered
1 small red onion (100g), sliced thickly
2 small yellow capsicums (300g)
2 small red capsicums (300g)
100g low-fat fetta cheese, crumbled
1 tablespoon finely shredded
  fresh basil
9 sheets fillo pastry
cooking-oil spray

1. Preheat oven to moderately hot.
2. Combine tomato and onion in baking dish; roast in hot oven, uncovered, about 30 minutes or until onion softens.
3. Meanwhile, quarter capsicums; remove and discard seeds and membranes. Roast under grill or in very hot oven, skin-side up, until skin blisters and blackens; cover capsicum pieces with plastic or paper 5 minutes. Peel away skin; slice capsicum thinly. Place capsicum, cheese and basil in baking dish with tomato mixture; stir gently to combine.
4. Stack sheets of fillo; spray with cooking-oil spray every third sheet. Carefully fold over all four edges of the stack to create 18cm x 30cm tart "shell".
5. Fill tart shell with vegetable mixture, spreading it to an even thickness; bake, uncovered, in moderately hot oven about 15 minutes or until pasty is browned lightly.

serves 6

per serving 4.4g fat; 450kJ

tip Keep fillo covered with a damp tea towel to prevent the sheets from drying out before use.

Serve with a salad of mixed baby greens, tossed with a splash of balsamic vinegar.

scallops in a fennel sabayon

preparation time 10 minutes • cooking time 20 minutes

An emulsion of egg yolk and wine creates a sauce which is light and creamy, yet low in fat and kilojoules, to accompany grilled scallops. We used scallops with the roe on but you can discard it if you prefer.

A sabayon is usually a dessert sauce — think of zabaglione. Here, we've made a savoury version by eliminating the sugar and adding the piquancy of lemon juice.

1 small fennel (300g), trimmed, sliced thinly
1 small leek (200g), sliced thinly
6 black peppercorns
1/3 cup (80ml) white wine vinegar
1/3 cup (80ml) dry white wine
32 scallops
2 egg yolks
2 tablespoons sparkling white wine
1 teaspoon lemon juice
1/3 cup (80ml) light cream
1 tablespoon finely chopped fresh dill

1. Using vegetable peeler, shave fennel into thin strips. Combine half of the fennel with leek, peppercorns, vinegar and dry wine in small saucepan; reserve remaining fennel. Bring wine mixture to a boil; reduce heat. Simmer, uncovered, until mixture reduces to about 2 tablespoons. Strain wine reduction into large heatproof bowl; discard solids. Cool slightly.
2. Cook scallops, in batches, on heated oiled grill plate (or grill or barbecue) until browned both sides and cooked as desired.
3. Place wine reduction with yolks, sparkling wine and juice in large bowl over large saucepan of simmering water; whisk yolks until mixture doubles in volume. Gradually whisk in cream; stir dill through mixture.
4. Drizzle serving plates with sauce; top with scallops and remaining fennel.

serves 8

per serving 4.5g fat; 367kJ

tip Make sauce immediately before serving, to prevent it losing volume.

serving suggestion Accompany scallops with the sparkling white wine you opened to make the sauce.

leek, spinach and mushroom frittata

preparation time 15 minutes • cooking time 40 minutes

This Italian interpretation of a low-fat vegetable omelette simplifies the cooking process by oven-baking, rather than completing it on the stove-top.

1 teaspoon low-fat dairy-free spread
3 cloves garlic, crushed
1 small leek (200g), sliced thinly
400g button mushrooms, sliced thickly
200g baby spinach leaves
2 eggs
6 egg whites
1/2 cup (125ml) skim milk
1/3 cup (40g) coarsely grated low-fat
   cheddar cheese

1. Preheat oven to moderately slow.
2. Oil deep 23cm-round cake pan. Line base with baking paper.
3. Melt dairy-free spread in medium frying pan; cook garlic and leek, stirring, until leek softens. Add mushrooms; cook, stirring, until mushrooms are just tender. Add spinach; cook, stirring, until spinach just wilts. Drain off and discard any liquid.
4. Using whisk, combine eggs, egg whites, milk and cheese in large bowl; stir in vegetable mixture.
5. Pour egg mixture into prepared pan. Bake in moderately slow oven about 30 minutes or until just set. Place frittata under hot grill until browned.

serves 6

per serving 3.0g fat; 380kJ

tip Use swiss brown mushrooms as an alternative tasty mushroom.

serving suggestion Serve with a salad of sliced tomatoes and shredded basil.

pureed parsnip and bean soup

preparation time 15 minute • cooking time 30 minutes

Many varieties of already cooked white beans are available canned, among them cannellini, butter and haricot beans; any of these are suitable for this salad. We used small cannellini beans in this recipe.

4 large parsnips (720g), chopped coarsely
1 cup (250ml) water
1 clove garlic, crushed
20g butter
2 x 400g cans white beans, drained, rinsed
1 litre (4 cups) chicken stock
1 cup (250ml) buttermilk

1. Preheat oven to hot.
2. Combine parsnip, the water, garlic and butter in medium baking dish; roast, uncovered, in hot oven about 15 minutes or until parsnip is tender.
3. Transfer parsnip mixture to large saucepan. Add beans and stock; bring to a boil. Reduce heat; simmer, uncovered, 10 minutes.
4. Blend or process soup, in batches, until smooth.
5. Return soup to cleaned pan. Add buttermilk; stir over low heat until hot.

serves 8

per serving 3.7g fat; 556kJ

serving suggestion Sprinkle soup with finely chopped chives and serve with warmed sourdough bread.

If you have time to soak and cook them, use dried white beans. You need about 1²/₃ cups (330g) dried beans to make the equivalent of two cans of beans.

creamy corn cake with salsa

preparation time 20 minutes • cooking time 30 minutes

The energy and fat counts on this pared-down version of an omelette prove that they don't have to be kilojoule-laden to be deliciously satisfying.

1 egg yolk
1/2 cup (75g) self-raising flour
420g can corn kernels, rinsed, drained
310g can creamed corn
2 egg whites

AVOCADO SALSA

500g cherry tomatoes, quartered
1 small avocado (200g),
    chopped coarsely
1 small red onion (100g),
    chopped finely
2 tablespoons coarsely chopped
    fresh coriander
2 tablespoons coarsely chopped
    fresh mint
1/4 cup (60ml) lime juice

1. Preheat oven to hot. Oil deep 23cm-round cake pan; line base and side with baking paper.
2. Combine egg yolk, flour, corn kernels and creamed corn in medium bowl. Beat egg whites in small bowl with electric mixer until soft peaks form; fold into yolk mixture.
3. Spread mixture into prepared pan; bake, uncovered, in hot oven about 30 minutes or until browned lightly and cooked through. Cut cake into eight wedges; serve with avocado salsa.
avocado salsa Combine ingredients in small bowl; toss gently.

serves 8

per serving 5.5g fat; 677kJ

tip If you omit the avocado from the salsa, the fat count will be significantly lower.

serving suggestion Serve with sambal oelek or add some finely chopped chilli to the salsa for a bit more spice.

tomato tarte tatin

preparation time 20 minutes • cooking time 1 hour (plus standing time)

The French sisters Tatin, who are credited with the invention of the apple version of this upside-down tart, would no doubt approve of their recipe's savoury incarnation.

2 large red onions (400g), sliced thinly
2 cups (440g) raw sugar
1/2 cup (125ml) balsamic vinegar
12 medium egg tomatoes
   (900g), halved
1 tablespoon water
2 sheets ready-rolled puff pastry
   with canola oil

Peppery baby rocket leaves tossed in a balsamic vinaigrette provide a bitey foil to the sweetness of this tarte.

1. Preheat oven to moderately hot.
2. Heat large lightly oiled non-stick frying pan; cook onion, stirring, until onion softens. Add 1 tablespoon of the sugar and vinegar to pan; cook, stirring, until onion caramelises.
3. Place tomatoes, cut-side up, in single layer on oven tray; bake, uncovered, in moderately hot oven about 20 minutes or until softened and browned lightly.
4. Meanwhile, lightly oil eight 10cm pie dishes. Combine remaining sugar with the water in large heavy-based saucepan; stir over low heat to combine. Cook, shaking pan constantly and stirring occasionally, until mixture crystallises. Continue cooking, stirring occasionally until mixture turns to a thick, dark syrup. Divide sugar mixture among pie dishes. Arrange three tomato halves, cut-side down, in each dish; top with onion mixture.
5. Cut four 10cm-rounds from each pastry sheet; top each dish with pastry round. Bake tarts, uncovered, in moderately hot oven about 15 minutes or until pastry is browned lightly; stand tarts for 2 minutes before turning onto serving plates.

serves 8

per serving 9.6g fat; 1661kJ

tip Don't worry when the sugar and water mixture turns to dry crystals. As you continue cooking, it will liquefy and become a toffee-like mixture.

char-grilled tuna with mixed vegetable stir-fry

preparation time 15 minutes (plus refrigeration time) • cooking time 10 minutes

The Italian hand-operated cutter and slicer, called a mandoline, is a useful kitchen tool to own if you make a lot of chips, or simply like to see precision-cut vegetables or fruits.

Tuna is best when seared both sides and fairly rare in the centre: overcooking can render this fish dry and unpalatable.

1/4 cup (60ml) sweet chilli sauce
1/4 cup (60ml) lime juice
1 tablespoon finely chopped
   fresh coriander
6 x 200g tuna steaks
2 tablespoons finely grated lime rind
1 red thai chilli, seeded, chopped finely
1 clove garlic, crushed
2 medium zucchini (240g)
2 medium carrots (240g)
2 medium red capsicums (400g),
   sliced thinly
1 medium yellow capsicum (200g),
   sliced thinly
1 small red onion (100g), sliced thinly

1. Combine chilli sauce, 2 teaspoons of the juice and coriander in small bowl.
2. Combine remaining juice in large bowl with tuna, rind, thai chilli and garlic. Cover; refrigerate 1 hour.
3. Meanwhile, using mandoline, V-slicer or sharp knife, cut zucchini and carrots into very thin slices; cut slices into matchstick-sized pieces.
4. Drain tuna; cook, in batches, on heated lightly oiled grill plate (or grill or barbecue) until browned both sides and cooked as desired.
5. Meanwhile, heat oiled wok or large non-stick frying pan; cook 1 tablespoon of the chilli sauce mixture, zucchini, carrot, capsicums and onion, in batches, until vegetables are just tender.
6. Serve tuna on vegetables; drizzle with remaining chilli sauce mixture.

serves 6

per serving 12.0g fat; 1517kJ

serving suggestion Accompany with rice vermicelli.

menu suggestion
begin with *pea flapjacks with smoked trout* page 6
follow with *crepes and strawberries with caramelised cointreau sauce* page 90

mains

seafood soup with garlic toast

preparation time 10 minutes • cooking time 1 hour

Prawns and pipis can also be added to the seafood content of this aromatic soup. We used thin bream fillets in this recipe but you can choose any firm white fish fillets that you like.

2 tablespoons olive oil
2 large brown onions (400g), chopped finely
3 cloves garlic, crushed
1/4 cup (70g) tomato paste
2 x 400g cans tomatoes
1/2 teaspoon ground saffron
1 tablespoon sugar
4 dried bay leaves
2 teaspoons coarsely chopped fresh thyme
1 cup (250ml) dry white wine
3 litres (12 cups) fish stock
2 tablespoons lemon juice
24 medium black mussels (600g)
200g scallops
400g white fish fillet, chopped coarsely
250g baby spinach leaves, shredded coarsely

GARLIC TOAST

1 long french bread stick
60g low-fat dairy-free spread
1 clove garlic, crushed
pinch cayenne pepper

1. Heat oil in large saucepan; cook onion and garlic, stirring, until onion softens. Add paste, undrained crushed tomatoes, saffron, sugar, bay leaves, thyme, wine, stock and juice; bring to a boil. Reduce heat; simmer, uncovered, about 45 minutes or until mixture reduces by half.
2. Meanwhile, scrub mussels under running water; remove beards.
3. Add mussels to soup; bring to a boil. Cook, covered, about 5 minutes or until mussels open (discard any that do not). Add scallops, fish and spinach; cook, uncovered, about 2 minutes or until fish is just tender. Serve seafood soup with garlic toast.

garlic toast Slice bread stick into 1cm slices. Combine dairy-free spread, garlic and cayenne pepper in small bowl. Spread mixture on bread slices; toast bread, both sides, under preheated grill.

serves 8

per serving 11.7g fat; 1512kJ

serving suggestion Sprinkle with finely shredded fresh basil just before serving.

menu suggestion
begin with *leek and asparagus risotto* page 20
follow with *banana pudding with espresso syrup* page 95

Thyme is much used in the food found along Europe's Mediterranean coastline, particularly in seafood soups and stews.

blue-eye char-grilled with dukkah and pilaf

preparation time 20 minutes • cooking time 45 minutes

Dukkah is an Egyptian nut, seed and spice mixture used similarly to Lebanese za'atar, Moroccan ras al hanout and Indian garam masala. It adds exotically complex, uniquely aromatic flavours to various grilled, baked or barbecued seafood, meat and poultry dishes. Each blend is slightly different, depending on the individual cook. Dukkah can also be used in a dip or sprinkled over a finished dish just before serving.

2 tablespoons hazelnut meal
2 tablespoons almond meal
1 tablespoon sesame seeds
1 tablespoon coriander seeds, crushed
1 tablespoon ground cumin
1 tablespoon sweet paprika
2 teaspoons ground turmeric
2 large red onions (600g)
800g flat mushrooms, quartered
6 cloves garlic
2 tablespoons olive oil
100g vermicelli, broken roughly
2 cups (400g) long-grain white rice
1 litre (4 cups) boiling water
8 x 150g blue-eye fillets
200g low-fat yogurt
1 tablespoon coarsely chopped
   fresh coriander
1 tablespoon lemon juice

1. Preheat oven to moderately hot.
2. Heat medium frying-pan; cook nuts, seeds and spices, stirring, until dukkah mixture is fragrant.
3. Cut each onion into six wedges; combine onion in large baking dish with mushrooms, garlic and half of the oil. Roast, uncovered, in moderately hot oven about 30 minutes or until vegetables are just tender.
4. Meanwhile, heat remaining oil in large saucepan with tight-fitting lid; cook vermicelli and rice, stirring, about 5 minutes or until vermicelli is golden brown and rice almost translucent. Add the water; bring to a boil. Reduce heat; simmer, covered, about 20 minutes or until liquid is absorbed and pilaf is cooked as desired.
5. While pilaf is cooking, coat fish all over in dukkah; cook, in batches, on heated oiled grill plate (or grill or barbecue) until browned both sides and cooked as desired.
6. Serve pilaf with fish and roasted vegetables; drizzle with combined yogurt, coriander and juice.

serves 8
per serving 12.8g fat; 2159kJ

menu suggestion
begin with *lamb fillo triangles* page 10
follow with *pink grapefruit souffles*
page 102

Egyptian households use dukkah as is, uncooked, by dipping pieces of bread first into a bowl of olive oil and then into the blended spice mixture.

garlic prawns and bok choy with herbed rice

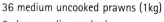

preparation time 20 minutes • cooking time 15 minutes

Traditional garlic prawns are given a Southeast-Asian tweak in this stir-fry.

36 medium uncooked prawns (1kg)

6 cloves garlic, crushed

2 teaspoons finely chopped
fresh coriander

3 red thai chillies, seeded,
chopped finely

1/3 cup (80ml) lime juice

1 teaspoon sugar

1 tablespoon peanut oil

1kg baby bok choy,
quartered lengthways

6 green onions, sliced thinly

1 tablespoon sweet chilli sauce

HERBED RICE

2 cups (400g) jasmine rice

2 tablespoons coarsely chopped
fresh coriander

1 tablespoon coarsely chopped
fresh mint

1 tablespoon coarsely chopped fresh
flat-leaf parsley

1 teaspoon finely grated lime rind

1. Shell and devein prawns, leaving tails intact.

2. Combine prawns in large bowl with garlic, coriander, chilli, juice and sugar.

3. Heat half of the oil in wok or large non-stick frying pan; stir-fry prawns, in batches, until just changed in colour.

4. Heat remaining oil with pan liquids in wok; stir-fry bok choy, onion and sauce, in batches, until just tender. Combine bok choy mixture and prawns in wok; stir-fry until hot. Serve prawns on herbed rice.

herbed rice Cook rice, uncovered, in large saucepan of boiling water until tender; drain. Return rice to pan; combine with remaining ingredients.

serves 6

per serving 4.5g fat; 1602kJ

menu suggestion
begin with *chicken wonton soup* page 8
follow with *peach galette* page 107

*Bok choy has become as common a
vegetable staple as green beans or
broccoli in most kitchens, and not
without good reason. It's versatile, easy
to cook, keeps well... and is delicious.*

farfalle with baked salmon, caperberries and dill

preparation time 25 minutes • cooking time 30 minutes

Farfalle is a classic short, dense pasta that is variously called bow ties or butterflies in English. Its frilled edges and soft pleats help contain sauce; substitute orecchiette (little ears) or fusilli (spirals or corkscrews) if preferred.

2 large red onions (600g)
1 cup (160g) caperberries, rinsed, drained
cooking-oil spray
1 red thai chilli, seeded, chopped finely
1/4 cup loosely packed, finely chopped fresh dill
2 teaspoons olive oil
1kg piece skinless salmon fillet
500g farfalle
2/3 cup (150ml) dry white wine
2 tablespoons lemon juice
1/2 cup (125ml) light cream
250g baby rocket leaves, trimmed

1. Preheat oven to moderately hot.
2. Cut each onion into eight wedges; place, in single layer, in large baking dish with caperberries. Spray lightly with cooking-oil spray; roast, uncovered, in moderately hot oven about 25 minutes or until onion is just softened.
3. Meanwhile, combine chilli and half of the dill in small bowl with olive oil. Place salmon on large baking-paper lined oven tray; brush salmon both sides with chilli mixture. Roast, uncovered, in moderately hot oven about 10 minutes or until salmon is just tender and cooked as desired.
4. Cook pasta, uncovered, in large saucepan of boiling water until just tender. While pasta is cooking, combine wine and juice in small saucepan; bring to a boil. Reduce heat; simmer, uncovered, about 5 minutes or until liquid reduces by half. Add cream and remaining dill.
5. Place pasta, flaked salmon, onion mixture and dill cream sauce in large bowl with baby rocket leaves; toss gently to combine.

serves 8

per serving 15.0g fat; 2090kJ

serving suggestions Sprinkle with freshly ground pepper and finely chopped chives.

menu suggestion
begin with *watercress salad* page 17
follow with *chocolate mousse* page 98

Caperberries are the fruit of the same Mediterranean shrub that produces the small flowerbuds we know as capers. About the size of a small olive, caperberries are sold pickled in vinegar; rinse and drain before use.

salmon patties with baby spinach

preparation time 30 minutes • cooking time 45 minutes

Baby spinach leaves, along with baby rocket, are the greens of choice for many people today. And why not? They can be used in everything from salads to stir-fries to soups, with no preparation or pre-cooking required; they're full of nutrients; and their respective singular flavours add something special to the dishes in which they are used.

5 medium potatoes (1kg), chopped coarsely
415g can red salmon, drained, flaked
6 green onions, chopped finely
2 trimmed sticks celery (150g), grated coarsely
1 teaspoon finely grated lemon rind
1/3 cup (80ml) lemon juice
2 egg whites
2 tablespoons water
2 cups (200g) packaged breadcrumbs
1 teaspoon vegetable oil
230g can sliced water chestnuts, drained
600g baby spinach leaves
1 tablespoon light soy sauce
1/4 cup (60ml) mirin
2 teaspoons sugar

1. Preheat oven to very hot.
2. Boil, steam or microwave potato until tender; drain. Mash potato in large bowl until smooth; cool slightly. Stir in salmon, onion, celery, rind and half of the juice.
3. Using floured hands, shape fish mixture into 16 patties. Dip patties, one at a time, in combined egg white and water, then in breadcrumbs. Place patties on lightly oiled oven tray. Cover; refrigerate 30 minutes.
4. Cook patties, uncovered, in very hot oven about 30 minutes or until golden brown and heated through.
5. Meanwhile, heat oil in wok or large non-stick frying pan; stir-fry water chestnuts 1 minute. Add spinach, remaining juice, sauce, mirin and sugar; stir-fry until spinach just wilts. Top spinach with salmon patties to serve.

serves 8

per serving 7.2g fat; 1203kJ

serving suggestion Accompany patties and spinach with tomato or sweet onion relish and sliced light rye bread.

menu suggestion
begin with *creamy corn omelette with salsa* page 29
follow with *banana pudding with espresso syrup* page 95

curried pork stir-fry with wild rice

preparation time 15 minutes • cooking time 15 minutes

2 cups (400g) basmati rice

1/2 cup (90g) wild rice

800g pork fillets, sliced thinly

2 teaspoons vegetable oil

2 cloves garlic, crushed

1 teaspoon grated fresh ginger

1 teaspoon ground coriander

1 teaspoon ground cumin

1 teaspoon ground turmeric

2 teaspoons garam masala

500g brussels sprouts, halved

300g patty-pan squash, quartered

1 medium leek (350g), sliced thinly

1/4 cup (60ml) lemon juice

1/4 cup (60ml) water

200g low-fat yogurt

1 tablespoon finely chopped fresh mint

1 tablespoon finely chopped
   fresh coriander

1/2 cup (140g) low-fat yogurt, extra

1. Cook rices, in separate medium saucepans of boiling water, until each is just tender (wild rice will take longer to cook than basmati); drain. Combine rices in large bowl; cover to keep warm.

2. Meanwhile, heat wok or large non-stick frying pan; stir-fry pork, in batches, until browned all over.

3. Heat oil in wok; stir-fry garlic, ginger and spices until fragrant. Add sprouts, squash, leek, juice and the water; stir-fry until vegetables are just tender.

4. Return pork to wok with yogurt and fresh herbs; stir-fry, tossing until combined.

5. Serve pork stir-fry with rice; drizzle with extra yogurt.

serves 6

per serving 5.3g fat; 2210kJ

menu suggestion

begin with *smoked chicken salad* page 14
follow with *lime cheesecake* page 96

You can replace the two individual rices in this recipe with one of the commercial blends of basmati and wild rice available in some supermarkets; cook a 500g package of the combined rices according to the manufacturer's instructions on the packet.

tuna and white bean salad

preparation time 15 minutes • cooking time 5 minutes

Canned cooked white beans can have one of several different names on the label - for instance, cannellini, butter or haricot. There is little difference in taste or texture among any of these small, slightly kidney-shaped white beans, and any would be suitable for this salad.

2 x 300g cans white beans, drained, rinsed

425g can tuna in springwater, drained, flaked

1 medium red onion (170g), sliced thinly

1/2 cup firmly packed, coarsely chopped fresh flat-leaf parsley

1 tablespoon coarsely chopped fresh oregano

250g cherry tomatoes, quartered

2 tablespoons olive oil

1 tablespoon white vinegar

2 teaspoons finely grated lemon rind

2 tablespoons lemon juice

2 cloves garlic, crushed

1 long loaf pide

1. Combine beans and tuna in large bowl with onion, parsley, oregano and tomato; toss gently with combined oil, vinegar, rind, juice and garlic.

2. Quarter bread crossways; slice pieces in half horizontally. Cut bread again, on the diagonal, to make 16 triangles; toast triangles, cut-side up.

3. Place one triangle, toasted-side up, on each serving plate; top with salad, then remaining triangles.

serves 8

per serving 7.4g fat; 1098kJ

menu suggestion
begin with *mussel chowder* page 12
follow with *black forest parfaits* page 94

Toss together equal amounts of baby rocket and baby spinach leaves with a lemon dressing to accompany this dish.

lime and chilli fish baked in banana leaves

preparation time 25 minutes • cooking time 15 minutes

Let your guests unwrap their own fish "package" at the table so that the spicy aroma wafts up from the plates and enlivens their appetites. Foil can be used if banana leaves are unavailable.

2 large banana leaves
4 stalks lemon grass
4 red thai chillies, seeded, sliced thinly
4 cloves garlic, crushed
1 tablespoon finely grated lime rind
1/3 cup (80ml) lime juice
2 tablespoons grated fresh ginger
1 cup loosely packed, coarsely chopped fresh coriander
1 cup (250ml) light coconut milk
8 x 150g ling fillets
cooking-oil spray
2 cups (400g) jasmine rice
4 green onions, sliced thinly

1. Preheat oven to hot.
2. Trim each banana leaf into four 30cm squares. Using metal tongs, dip one square at a time into large saucepan of boiling water; remove immediately. Rinse under cold running water; pat dry with absorbent paper. Banana leaf squares should be soft and pliable.
3. Halve lemon grass stalks. Combine chilli, garlic, rind, juice, ginger, coriander and coconut milk in small bowl.
4. Centre each fillet on banana leaf square. Top with lemon grass; drizzle with chilli mixture. Fold square over fish to enclose; secure each parcel with kitchen string.
5. Place parcels, in single layer, in large baking dish; coat with cooking-oil spray. Roast in hot oven about 10 minutes or until fish is cooked as desired.
6. Meanwhile, cook rice, uncovered, in large saucepan of boiling water until tender; drain. Stir onion through rice; serve with unwrapped fish parcels.

serves 8

per serving 7.0g fat; 1592kJ

serving suggestion Accompany with a small bowl of thai sweet chilli sauce.

menu suggestion
begin with *oven-baked spring rolls* page 18
follow with *poached nashi in asian-spiced syrup* page 100

Many supermarkets and greengrocers sell bundles of trimmed banana-leaf squares; they can also be used as placemats for a Southeast-Asian meal.

pork rissoles on potato rösti with leek puree

preparation time 30 minutes • cooking time 45 minutes

Comfort food at its multifaceted finest… perfect for the family or for special guests.

1kg lean pork mince

2 cloves garlic, crushed

1 medium brown onion (150g), chopped finely

1/2 cup firmly packed, coarsely chopped fresh mint

1 egg white, beaten lightly

1 cup (70g) stale breadcrumbs

5 medium potatoes (1kg)

1/4 cup (35g) plain flour

1 egg white, beaten lightly, extra

2 large leeks (1kg), chopped coarsely

2 tablespoons skim milk

1. Preheat oven to hot.

2. Combine pork, garlic, onion, mint, egg white and breadcrumbs in large bowl. Using hands, shape pork mixture into 18 patties; place on lightly oiled tray. Cover; refrigerate 30 minutes.

3. Meanwhile, peel and coarsely grate potatoes; using hand, squeeze out excess liquid. Combine potato, flour and extra egg white in large bowl. Using hands, shape potato mixture into 12 patties. Place potato rösti, in single layer, on lightly oiled oven trays; bake, uncovered, turning once, in hot oven about 30 minutes or until rösti are browned both sides.

4. Heat large oiled heavy-based saucepan; cook leek, stirring, until softened. Blend or process leek with milk until mixture forms a thick puree.

5. Meanwhile, heat large oiled non-stick frying pan; cook rissoles, in batches, until browned both sides and cooked through.

6. Stack three patties and two rösti on each serving plate; top with leek puree.

serves 6

per serving 3.8g fat; 1590kJ

tip Brown onions can be substituted for leeks, if preferred.

menu suggestion
begin with *roasted pumpkin, sesame and rocket salad* page 9
follow with *pear and ginger cake* page 92

Common garden mint, a variety of spearmint, makes a good salad ingredient, but it should only be added just before serving because the leaves blacken rapidly once they've been chopped or shredded.

pepper-grilled lamb fillets with roasted root vegetables

preparation time 30 minutes • cooking time 1 hour

All manner of baby vegetables are available at better greengrocers and some supermarkets. You could also serve baby cauliflower, baby turnips and baby pumpkin with the lamb in this recipe.

1kg baby beetroots, trimmed
6 small parsnips (360g), quartered
500g baby new potatoes, halved
400g baby carrots, trimmed
8 baby onions (200g), halved
4 cloves garlic, peeled
$1/4$ cup (60ml) orange juice
$1/4$ cup (90g) honey
1 tablespoon seeded mustard
12 lamb fillets (960g)
$1 1/2$ tablespoons cracked black pepper

1. Preheat oven to moderately hot.
2. Boil, steam or microwave unpeeled beetroot until tender; drain. When cool enough to handle, peel beetroot.
3. Combine beetroot in large lightly oiled baking dish with parsnip, potato, carrot, onion and garlic. Pour combined juice, honey and mustard over vegetables; roast, uncovered, in moderately hot oven, stirring occasionally, about 45 minutes or until vegetables are browned and tender.
4. Meanwhile, coat lamb all over with pepper. Cook lamb on heated oiled grill plate (or grill or barbecue) until browned all over and cooked as desired. Cover; stand 10 minutes. Slice thickly.
5. Serve vegetables topped with lamb.

serves 8
per serving 4.8g fat; 1228kJ

menu suggestion
begin with *pea flapjacks with smoked trout* page 6
follow with *poached nashi in asian-spiced syrup* page 100

Accompany this recipe with bowl of lemon-scented steamed couscous.

lamb and apricot tagine with citrus couscous

preparation time 20 minutes (plus 45 minutes standing time) • cooking time 1 hour

A tagine is a Moroccan slow-cooked meat or vegetable stew that is traditionally served with warm couscous.

1²/3 cups (250g) dried apricots
3/4 cup (180ml) orange juice
1/2 cup (125ml) boiling water
2 tablespoons olive oil
900g lamb steaks, chopped coarsely
2 medium red capsicums (400g),
    chopped coarsely
1 large brown onion (200g),
    chopped coarsely
2 medium kumara (800g),
    chopped coarsely
3 cloves garlic, crushed
1 teaspoon ground cinnamon
2 teaspoons ground cumin
2 teaspoons ground coriander
1 cup (250ml) dry red wine
1 litre (4 cups) chicken stock
2 tablespoons honey
1 cup loosely packed fresh
    coriander leaves
200g low-fat yogurt

CITRUS COUSCOUS

1 litre (4 cups) water
4 cups (800g) couscous
1 tablespoon finely grated orange rind
2 teaspoons finely grated lemon rind
2 teaspoons finely grated lime rind

1. Combine apricots, juice and the water in small bowl. Cover; allow to stand 45 minutes.
2. Meanwhile, heat half of the oil in large saucepan; cook lamb, in batches, until browned all over.
3. Heat remaining oil in same pan; cook capsicum, onion, kumara, garlic and ground spices, stirring, until onion softens and mixture is fragrant. Add wine; bring to a boil. Reduce heat; simmer, uncovered, about 5 minutes or until liquid reduces by half.
4. Return lamb to pan with undrained apricots, stock and honey; bring to a boil. Reduce heat; simmer, covered, about 50 minutes or until lamb is tender. Remove from heat; stir in fresh coriander.
5. Serve lamb on citrus couscous; drizzle with yogurt.

citrus couscous Bring the water to a boil in medium saucepan; stir in couscous and rinds. Remove from heat; stand, covered, about 5 minutes or until liquid is absorbed, fluffing with fork occasionally to separate grains.

serves 8

per serving 12.8g fat;1837kJ

menu suggestion
begin with *gazpacho* page 15
follow with *grilled figs with cinnamon-scented ricotta* page 93

Accompany the tagine with a separate bowl of harissa, the spicy Moroccan condiment, to enliven it with heat.

lamb with harissa carrot puree

preparation time 10 minutes (plus standing time) • cooking time 25 minutes

While harissa, that exquisitely piquant blend of chilli, garlic, caraway and other spices, can be bought at nearly every supermarket these days, here we've made a delicious low-fat version without oil.

1 medium red capsicum (200g)
8 large carrots (1.5kg), chopped coarsely
40g low-fat dairy-free spread
2 red thai chillies, seeded, chopped coarsely
1 clove garlic, crushed
1 tablespoon ground cumin
1 tablespoon ground coriander
1 teaspoon caraway seeds
1 cup (250ml) buttermilk
1 tablespoon coarsely chopped fresh flat-leaf parsley
12 lamb fillets (960g)
2 teaspoons ground cumin, extra
2 teaspoons ground coriander, extra

1. Quarter capsicum; remove and discard seeds and membrane. Roast, under grill or in very hot oven, skin-side up, until skin blisters and blackens. Cover capsicum pieces in plastic or paper 5 minutes; peel away and discard skin. Chop capsicum coarsely.
2. Boil, steam or microwave carrot until tender. Drain; keep warm.
3. Heat dairy-free spread in small heavy-based saucepan; cook chilli, garlic, cumin, coriander and caraway, stirring, until chilli softens and harissa is fragrant. Stir in buttermilk; blend or process chilli-spice mixture with capsicum, carrot and parsley, in batches, until mixture forms a smooth puree.
4. Coat lamb, all over, with combined extra spices. Cook lamb, in batches, on heated oiled grill plate (or grill or barbecue) until browned all over and cooked as desired. Serve with harissa carrot puree.

serves 6

per serving 10.0g fat; 1274kJ

serving suggestion Accompany with a bowl of low-fat yogurt flavoured with chilli and mint.

menu suggestion
begin with *char-grilled polenta cakes* page 21
follow with *melon granita trio* page 104

lamb cutlets with potato and parsnip mash

preparation time 15 minutes (plus refrigeration time) • cooking time 20 minutes

18 french-trimmed lamb cutlets (1.4kg)
4 cloves garlic, crushed
2 teaspoons grated fresh ginger
1/4 cup coarsely chopped fresh mint
1/3 cup (80ml) balsamic vinegar
2 large potatoes (600g),
    chopped coarsely
5 medium parsnips (625g),
    chopped coarsely
1/2 cup (125ml) buttermilk
11/2 cups (375ml) vegetable stock

1. Combine lamb in large bowl with garlic, ginger, mint and half of the vinegar; toss to coat lamb all over. Cover; refrigerate 3 hours or overnight.
2. Boil, steam or microwave potato and parsnip until tender; drain. Mash potato and parsnip in large bowl with buttermilk until smooth.
3. Meanwhile, heat large lightly oiled non-stick frying pan; cook lamb, in batches, until browned both sides and cooked as desired. Cover to keep warm.
4. Add remaining vinegar and stock to same pan; bring to a boil. Reduce heat; simmer, uncovered, until sauce reduces by two-thirds. Serve lamb with mash; drizzle with strained sauce.

serves 6

per serving 11.8 fat; 1396kJ

serving suggestion Serve with thinly sliced ripe tomatoes drizzled with balsamic vinegar.

menu suggestion
begin with *mussel chowder* page 12
follow with *chocolate fudge cake*
page 99

pepper steak with scalloped potatoes

preparation time 15 minutes • cooking time 55 minutes

Recipe heaven: we show you how to make delicious scalloped potatoes without overdoing the fat component.

Serve with a platter of assorted crisp leafy vegetables - include radicchio for a spot of colour and its great flavour.

2 medium brown onions (300g), sliced thinly
2 cloves garlic, crushed
5 medium potatoes (1kg), sliced thinly
1/2 cup (120g) light sour cream
1/2 cup (125ml) chicken stock
1 cup (125g) coarsely grated low-fat cheddar cheese
6 beef fillet steaks (600g)
2 teaspoons cracked black pepper
1 clove garlic, crushed, extra
1 tablespoon cornflour
1 cup (250ml) beef stock

1. Preheat oven to moderate.
2. Heat large lightly oiled non-stick frying pan. Cook onion and garlic, stirring, until onion softens.
3. Layer onion mixture and potato in shallow 2.5 litre (10-cup) baking dish, finishing with potato layer. Pour combined sour cream and stock over potato mixture; sprinkle with cheese.
4. Bake potato mixture, covered, in moderate oven 45 minutes. Uncover; bake about 10 minutes or until scalloped potatoes are tender and browned lightly on top.
5. Meanwhile, coat beef all over with pepper; cook, in batches, in large heated lightly oiled non-stick frying pan until browned both sides and cooked as desired. Cover beef to keep warm.
6. Add extra garlic to same pan; cook, stirring, until fragrant. Blend cornflour with stock in small jug; add to pan. Stir over heat until sauce mixture boils and thickens slightly. Drizzle steaks with sauce; serve with scalloped potatoes.

serves 6

per serving 10.5g fat; 1124-kJ

menu suggestion
begin with *scallops in a fennel sabayon* page 26
follow with *rhubarb and strawberry sponge pudding* page 101

lamb kofta with chilli and yogurt sauce

preparation time 20 minutes • cooking time 10 minutes

You need 18 bamboo skewers for this recipe. Soak them in water for at least an hour before use to help prevent them from splintering or scorching.

Kofta can be finger-, ball- or torpedo-shaped but all are made of minced meat and spices, then hand-moulded before grilling.

1kg lean lamb mince
1 large brown onion (200g), chopped finely
1 clove garlic, crushed
1 tablespoon ground cumin
2 teaspoons ground turmeric
2 teaspoons ground allspice
1 tablespoon finely chopped fresh mint
2 tablespoons finely chopped fresh flat-leaf parsley
1 egg, beaten lightly
6 pocket pitta, quartered

YOGURT SAUCE

200g low-fat yogurt
1 clove garlic, crushed
1 tablespoon finely chopped fresh flat-leaf parsley

CHILLI TOMATO SAUCE

1/4 cup (60ml) tomato sauce
1/4 cup (60ml) chilli sauce

1. Using hands, combine lamb, onion, garlic, spices, herbs and egg in large bowl; shape mixture into 18 balls. Mould balls around skewers to form sausage shapes. Cook, in batches, on heated oiled grill plate (or grill or barbecue) until browned all over and cooked through.
2. Serve kofta with pitta, yogurt sauce and chilli tomato sauce.
yogurt sauce Combine yogurt, garlic and parsley in small bowl.
chilli tomato sauce Combine tomato and chilli sauces in small bowl.

serves 6
per serving 14.5g fat; 1817kJ

menu suggestion
begin with *roasted vegetable fillo tart* page 24
follow with *honey buttermilk ice-cream with fresh fruit salsa* page 105

Serve a large bowl of homemade tabbouleh – its dressing heavy on lemon juice and light on oil – with the kofta.

beef fajitas

preparation time 30 minutes • cooking time 20 minutes

You need a small iceberg lettuce for this recipe and 2 packets of small flour tortillas (sometimes labelled "fajita tortillas" on the package).

800g trimmed beef rump steak
1 large red capsicum (350g),
    sliced thinly
1 large green capsicum (350g),
    sliced thinly
1 large yellow capsicum (350g),
    sliced thinly
1 large red onion (300g), sliced thinly
16 small flour tortillas (16cm diameter)
3 cups finely shredded iceberg lettuce
1¹/₄ cups (155g) coarsely grated
    low-fat cheddar cheese

FRESH TOMATO SALSA

3 medium tomatoes (570g), seeded,
    chopped finely
1 medium red onion (170g),
    chopped finely
1 tablespoon finely chopped drained
    jalapeño chillies
¹/₄ cup firmly packed, finely chopped
    fresh coriander
1 tablespoon lemon juice

1. Heat large lightly oiled grill plate (or grill or barbecue). Sear beef both sides until browned and cooked as desired. Cover; stand 10 minutes. Slice thinly.
2. Meanwhile, on same grill plate, cook capsicums and onion, in batches, until vegetables are browned all over.
3. Heat tortillas in microwave oven or in pre-heated oven according to manufacturer's instructions on package.
4. Divide beef slices and vegetables among tortillas on serving plates. Top each with lettuce and cheese; roll to enclose filling. Serve with separate bowl of fresh tomato salsa.
fresh tomato salsa Combine ingredients in small bowl.

serves 8
per serving 9.0g fat; 1390kJ

menu suggestion
begin with *gazpacho* page 15
follow with *chocolate fudge cake*
page 99

Avocado is filled with the "good" oil so a little of it, mashed and spread on the tortilla before filling, won't do any harm.

artichoke and eggplant veal rolls

preparation time 20 minutes • cooking time 30 minutes

This is a quick and easy rendition of a traditional Sicilian involtini – slow-cooked meat rolls filled with vegetables served in a rich tomato sauce.

400g can artichokes, drained
3 green onions, chopped coarsely
1 clove garlic, quartered
1 medium eggplant (300g),
    sliced thinly
8 veal steaks (720g)
1 large brown onion (200g),
    chopped coarsely
2 medium red capsicums (400g),
    chopped coarsely
4 trimmed sticks celery (300g),
    chopped coarsely
4 small tomatoes (520g), seeded,
    chopped coarsely
1/2 cup (125ml) brandy
1/2 cup (125ml) beef stock
2 tablespoons tomato paste

1. Blend or process artichokes, onion and garlic until mixture forms a paste.
2. Heat large lightly oiled non-stick frying pan; cook eggplant, in batches, until browned both sides.
3. Place veal pieces on board; spread each with artichoke mixture then top with eggplant. Roll veal to enclose filling; secure each roll with toothpick or kitchen string.
4. Cook veal, in batches, in same pan until browned all over and cooked as desired. Cover veal rolls to keep warm.
5. Cook onion in same pan, stirring, until softened. Add capsicum, celery, tomato and brandy; cook, stirring, until vegetables are tender and pan liquid reduces by half. Add stock and tomato paste; cook, stirring, until mixture boils and thickens slightly.
6. Cut each veal roll into thirds. Place four of the thirds on each serving plate; top with vegetables and sauce.

serves 6
per serving 3.4g fat; 916 kJ

menu suggestion
begin with *pasta with fresh tomato sauce* page 22
follow with *guilt-free tiramisu* page 106

*Make some gremolata by combining
1/2 cup finely chopped flat-leaf parsley,
2 finely chopped garlic cloves and
1 tablespoon of finely chopped lemon rind
and sprinkle it over the veal at the table.*

fish and oven-roasted chips

preparation time 10 minutes • cooking time 45 minutes

Yes, it's true! You can make delicious fish and chips without using an extravagant amount of oil. We used bream fillets here but you can use other firm white fish fillets, such as whiting or john dory.

5 large potatoes (1.5kg)
1 teaspoon sea salt
1/2 teaspoon cracked black pepper
cooking-oil spray
6 x 120g white fish fillets
2 tablespoons drained baby capers
1 tablespoon finely chopped
   fresh dill
1 teaspoon finely grated lemon rind
1/3 cup (80ml) lemon juice

1. Preheat oven to hot. Halve unpeeled potatoes lengthways; cut each half into six wedges.
2. Combine potato, in single layer, in large baking dish with salt and pepper; spray lightly with cooking-oil spray. Roast, uncovered, in hot oven about 45 minutes or until chips are browned lightly and tender.
3. Meanwhile, cook fish, uncovered, in large heated lightly oiled non-stick frying pan until browned both sides and cooked as desired.
4. Drizzle combined remaining ingredients over fish just before serving; served fish and chips with lemon wedges, if desired.

serves 6

per serving 3.4g fat; 1137kJ

serving suggestion Individual garden salads in a light lemony vinaigrette are perfect with the fish and chips.

menu suggestion
begin with *steamed sweet chilli prawn dumplings* page 23
follow with *black forest parfaits* page 94

Baby capers are the young grey-green buds of a warm climate shrub available either dried and salted or pickled in vinegar; they are used to enhance sauces and dressings with their piquant flavour.

veal and fettuccine in sage mustard sauce

preparation time 10 minutes • cooking time 15 minutes

500g fettuccine
8 veal steaks (640g)
2 cloves garlic, crushed
2 tablespoons seeded mustard
3/4 cup (180ml) dry white wine
1 cup (250ml) chicken stock
2 teaspoons finely shredded fresh sage
300g snow peas, sliced thinly

1. Cook pasta in large saucepan of boiling water until just tender.
2. While pasta is cooking, cook veal, in batches, in large lightly oiled non-stick frying pan until browned both sides and cooked as desired; cover to keep warm.
3. Add garlic and mustard to same pan; cook, stirring, 1 minute. Add wine and stock; bring to a boil. Reduce heat; simmer, uncovered, about 5 minutes or until liquid reduces by half. Stir in sage.
4. Meanwhile, boil, steam or microwave snow peas until just tender; drain.
5. Cut veal pieces in half on the diagonal. Combine drained pasta and snow peas; divide among serving plates. Top with veal; drizzle with sage mustard sauce.

serves 8

per serving 2.9g fat; 1398kJ

serving suggestion Sprinkle pasta with tiny whole fresh sage leaves.

menu suggestion
begin with *baked ricotta with roasted capsicum salad* page 11
follow with *chocolate mousse* page 98

turkey and lemon risotto

preparation time 10 minutes • cooking time 40 minutes

2 litres (8 cups) chicken stock

1 cup (250ml) dry white wine

1/2 cup (125ml) lemon juice

2 teaspoons low-fat dairy-free spread

1 medium brown onion (150g),
  chopped finely

2 cloves garlic, crushed

4 cups (800g) arborio rice

1 1/2 cups (185g) frozen peas

6 turkey fillets (650g)

2 teaspoons finely grated lemon rind

2 teaspoons finely chopped
  fresh thyme

1/4 cup (20g) finely grated
  parmesan cheese

1. Combine stock, wine and juice in large saucepan; bring to a boil. Reduce heat; simmer, uncovered.

2. Heat dairy-free spread in separate large saucepan; cook onion and garlic, stirring, until onion softens. Add rice; stir to coat in spread mixture. Stir in 1 cup of the hot stock mixture; cook, stirring, over low heat until liquid is absorbed. Continue adding stock mixture, in 1-cup batches, stirring until absorbed between each addition. Add peas; cook 5 minutes. Total cooking time should be about 35 minutes.

3. Meanwhile, cook turkey, in batches, in large lightly oiled non-stick frying pan until browned both sides and cooked through; chop coarsely.

4. Gently stir turkey, rind, thyme and cheese into risotto.

serves 6

per serving 7.4g fat; 2943kJ

serving suggestion Serve with a green salad and warmed loaf of Italian bread.

tip Chicken breast fillets can be substituted for turkey fillets.

menu suggestion
begin with *roasted pumpkin, sesame and rocket salad* page 9
follow with *guilt-free tiramisu* page 106

creole chicken and dirty rice

preparation time 20 minutes • cooking time 45 minutes

This chicken recipe originated in the southern United States, where European cuisine merged with Haitian and African-American fare to create Creole dishes – the spicy, rich cooking style of Louisiana. As for the dirty rice, this classic recipe from the Deep South is so delicious that both Cajun and Creole cooks claim it as their own.

Now a staple in southern kitchens, okra wasn't known in America until it was farmed by African slaves, who brought seeds of this green-podded vegetable with them from their homeland.

1 medium brown onion (150g), chopped coarsely
1 clove garlic, crushed
2 bay leaves
1 teaspoon hot paprika
1/2 teaspoon cayenne pepper
1/2 teaspoon cracked black pepper
1 medium green capsicum (200g), chopped coarsely
3 trimmed sticks celery (225g), chopped coarsely
100g fresh okra, sliced thinly
2 x 400g cans tomatoes
500g chicken breast fillets, chopped coarsely

DIRTY RICE
1²/3 cups (330g) long-grain white rice
400g lean pork fillet
1 small green capsicum (150g), chopped finely
1 small brown onion (80g), chopped finely
1 trimmed stick celery (75g), chopped finely
1 teaspoon hot paprika
1/2 teaspoon mustard powder
1/4 teaspoon ground cumin
1 teaspoon finely chopped fresh thyme
1 teaspoon finely chopped fresh oregano
1 cup (250ml) water
1 cup (250ml) chicken stock

1. Heat large lightly oiled non-stick frying pan; cook onion, garlic, bay leaves and spices, stirring, until onion softens. Add capsicum, celery and okra; cook, stirring, until vegetables are just tender. Add undrained crushed tomatoes; bring to a boil. Reduce heat; simmer, uncovered, stirring occasionally, about 25 minutes or until vegetable mixture thickens slightly.
2. Add chicken to vegetable mixture; cook, uncovered, about 15 minutes or until chicken is cooked through. Serve chicken with dirty rice.
dirty rice Cook ²/3 cup of the rice, uncovered, in medium saucepan of boiling water, until tender. Drain; keep warm. Chop pork into fine slivers (or blend or process). Cook pork in large heated lightly oiled non-stick frying pan with capsicum, onion, celery, spices and herbs, stirring, until onion softens. Add remaining rice, the water and stock; bring to a boil. Reduce heat; simmer, covered, about 15 minutes or until rice is tender. Add cooked rice; toss gently until just combined.

serves 6
per serving 6.9g fat; 1840kJ

menu suggestion
begin with *watercress salad* page 17
follow with *rhubarb and strawberry sponge pudding* page 101

balsamic-glazed chicken breasts with tomato and basil couscous

preparation time 20 minutes • cooking time 30 minutes

The foods and flavours of Italy and Morocco mingle in this recipe, resulting in a uniquely mouthwatering meal.

8 medium tomatoes (1.5kg)
8 cloves garlic, sliced thinly
1 tablespoon olive oil
8 single chicken breast fillets (1.4kg)
1/2 cup (125ml) balsamic vinegar
2 tablespoons honey
1/4 cup (60ml) dry sherry
2 tablespoons seeded mustard
1 litre (4 cups) boiling water
4 cups (800g) couscous
20g butter
1 cup loosely packed, finely
  shredded fresh basil

1. Preheat oven to moderate.
2. Cut each tomato into eight wedges. Combine tomato, in single layer, with garlic and half of the oil in large shallow baking dish; roast, uncovered, in moderate oven 30 minutes.
3. Meanwhile, heat remaining oil in large non-stick frying pan; cook chicken, in batches, until lightly browned all over.
4. Place vinegar, honey, sherry and mustard in same pan; bring to a boil. Return chicken to pan; reduce heat. Simmer, uncovered, about 10 minutes or until chicken is cooked through.
5. Bring the water to a boil in medium saucepan; stir in couscous and butter. Remove from heat; stand, covered, about 5 minutes or until liquid is absorbed, fluffing with fork occasionally. Stir in tomato mixture and basil; toss with fork to combine. Serve chicken on couscous; drizzle with remaining pan juices.

serves 8

per serving 14.9g fat; 2958kJ

menu suggestion
begin with *low-fat caesar salad* page 16
follow with *pear and ginger cake* page 92

A large bowl of lightly steamed green and yellow string beans is a simple accompaniment for this recipe.

moroccan grilled chicken with beetroot puree and couscous

preparation time 30 minutes • cooking time 1 hour 15 minutes

Pureed beetroot takes on potato mash as one of the great accompaniments. You can also stir a bit more yogurt and a pinch of nutmeg into the beetroot puree to make a delectable dip for pitta crisps.

8 single chicken breast fillets (1.4kg)
1 tablespoon olive oil
2 teaspoons finely grated lemon rind
2 tablespoons lemon juice
2 cloves garlic, crushed
1 tablespoon ground coriander
1 tablespoon ground cumin
2 teaspoons ground cardamom
1 teaspoon sweet paprika
1 teaspoon ground turmeric
1/2 cup firmly packed, finely chopped fresh flat-leaf parsley
1/4 cup firmly packed, finely chopped fresh coriander
6 medium beetroot (1kg), trimmed
1/2 cup (140g) low-fat yogurt
2 cups (400g) couscous
2 cups (500ml) boiling water
1/4 cup firmly packed, finely chopped fresh mint

1. Preheat oven to moderate.
2. Combine chicken, oil, rind, juice, garlic, spices, parsley and fresh coriander in large bowl. Cover; refrigerate 1 hour.
3. Meanwhile, wrap unpeeled beetroot in foil. Place on oven tray; roast in moderate oven about 1 hour or until tender. When cool enough to handle, peel beetroot; chop coarsely then blend or process until pureed. Stir in yogurt; cover to keep warm.
4. Combine couscous and the water in large heatproof bowl. Cover; stand about 5 minutes or until the water is absorbed, fluffing couscous with fork occasionally to separate grains. Add mint; toss gently with fork to combine.
5. Cook undrained chicken, in batches, in large heated lightly oiled non-stick frying pan until browned both sides and cooked through. Serve chicken on couscous; top with beetroot puree.

serves 8

per serving 13.0g fat; 2133kJ

serving suggestion Serve with a simple mixed green salad.

menu suggestion
begin with *creamy corn omelette with salsa* page 29
follow with *peach galette* page 107

Cardamom pods should be bruised with the side of a heavy knife until crushed just to the point of opening; the seeds can then be extracted and used, whole or ground.

thai basil chicken stir-fry

preparation time 20 minutes (plus refrigeration time) • cooking time 20 minutes

The food of Thailand takes first prize in the popularity stakes these days and no wonder: quick and easy to prepare, delicious recipes like this one are every cook's dream… and their fresh vegetable content makes them healthy too. You'll need to grate the rind from the lime before you juice it.

1 teaspoon sesame oil
1/2 cup (125ml) light soy sauce
1/4 cup (75g) honey
1/4 cup (60ml) lime juice
3 red thai chillies, seeded, sliced thinly
2 teaspoons cornflour
850g chicken breast fillets, sliced thinly
2 tablespoons peanut oil
3 cloves garlic, crushed
2 large red onions (400g), sliced thinly
240g fresh baby corn
2 teaspoons finely grated lime rind
3 cups (240g) bean sprouts
2 cups loosely packed fresh thai basil leaves
1 cup loosely packed fresh coriander leaves

1. Combine sesame oil, sauce, honey, juice, chilli and cornflour in large bowl. Add chicken; toss to coat in marinade. Cover; refrigerate 3 hours or overnight.
2. Drain chicken over medium bowl; reserve marinade.
3. Heat half of the peanut oil in wok or large non-stick frying pan; stir-fry chicken, in batches, until browned all over. Heat remaining peanut oil in wok; stir-fry garlic, onion and corn until just tender. Return chicken to wok with reserved marinade and rind; stir-fry until sauce boils and chicken is cooked through.
4. Remove from heat; add sprouts, basil and coriander. Toss with chicken and vegetables until combined.

serves 8

per serving 11.5g fat; 1183kJ

serving suggestion Serve with steamed jasmine rice and wedges of fresh lime.

menu suggestion
begin with *oven-baked spring rolls* page 18
follow with *melon granita trio* page 104

Also known as bai kaprow or holy basil, thai basil has slightly smaller leaves than common basil and a strong, somewhat bitter, flavour.

chicken scaloppine with gremolata

preparation time 30 minutes • cooking time 30 minutes

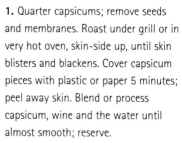

Gremolata is to osso buco what thousand island dressing is to prawn cocktail – you can't have one without the other. But this finely chopped blend of lemon rind, garlic and parsley is far too good to save for just the odd veal shank or two.. and it's very well-suited to chicken.

2 large red capsicums (600g)
1/2 cup (125ml) dry white wine
1/2 cup (125ml) water
2 cups firmly packed, coarsely chopped fresh flat-leaf parsley
2 tablespoons coarsely grated lemon rind
2 tablespoons lemon juice
2 cloves garlic, quartered
8 single chicken breast fillets (1.4kg)
8 slices prosciutto (120g)

1. Quarter capsicums; remove seeds and membranes. Roast under grill or in very hot oven, skin-side up, until skin blisters and blackens. Cover capsicum pieces with plastic or paper 5 minutes; peel away skin. Blend or process capsicum, wine and the water until almost smooth; reserve.
2. Preheat oven to moderate. Blend or process parsley, rind, juice and garlic until gremolata is almost smooth.
3. Cut chicken fillets in half horizontally almost all the way through; open out each fillet. Place between sheets of plastic wrap; pound gently with meat mallet until about 1cm thick. Divide gremolata among fillets; roll each fillet to enclose filling. Wrap each roll in prosciutto; secure with toothpicks.
4. Place chicken rolls in large oiled shallow baking dish; bake, uncovered, in moderate oven about 30 minutes or until chicken is cooked through.
5. Meanwhile, place capsicum mixture in small saucepan; bring to a boil. Reduce heat; simmer, uncovered, about 3 minutes or until reduced by half. Add pan juices from chicken; return to a boil. Serve chicken on capsicum sauce.

serves 8

per serving 10.7g fat; 1200kJ

menu suggestion
begin with *lamb fillo triangles* page 10
follow with *grilled figs with cinnamon-scented ricotta* page 93

Serve with boiled baby new potatoes tossed with lemon juice and finely chopped fresh flat-leaf parsley.

spanish-style chicken

preparation time 20 minutes • cooking time 45 minutes

Chicken drummettes are drumsticks with the end of the bone chopped off. They are also sold as "lovely legs".

2 teaspoons olive oil
1 large brown onion (200g), chopped coarsely
2 cloves garlic, crushed
2 medium green capsicums (400g), chopped coarsely
16 chicken drummettes (2kg)
410g can tomato puree
1 teaspoon hot paprika
1 tablespoon ground coriander
1 tablespoon ground cumin
1/2 teaspoon cayenne pepper
2 cups (320g) fresh corn kernels
1/2 cup (125ml) dry red wine
1 cup (250ml) chicken stock
2 bay leaves
1 1/2 cups (300g) long-grain white rice
2 tablespoons finely chopped fresh flat-leaf parsley

1. Preheat oven to moderately hot.
2. Heat oil in large flameproof baking dish with tight-fitting lid; cook onion, garlic and capsicum, stirring, until vegetables just soften. Remove vegetables, leaving as much oil in dish as possible. Add chicken, in batches, to dish; cook until browned all over.
3. Return chicken and vegetables to dish with tomato puree, spices, corn, wine, stock, bay leaves and rice; bring to a boil. Cover tightly; cook in oven about 30 minutes or until rice is tender and chicken cooked through. Sprinkle with parsley just before serving.

serves 8

per serving 12.0g fat; 1800kJ

serving suggestion Serve with plenty of warm crunchy bread rolls.

menu suggestion
begin with *baked ricotta with roasted capsicum salad* page 11
follow with *honey buttermilk ice-cream with fresh fruit salsa* page 105

grilled paprika chicken with raisin and coriander pilaf

preparation time 20 minutes (plus refrigeration time) • cooking time 40 minutes

8 skinless chicken thigh cutlets (1.3kg)
2 tablespoons lemon juice
3 cloves garlic, crushed
1/2 teaspoon hot paprika
1 teaspoon sweet paprika
1 teaspoon ground cinnamon
200g low-fat yogurt
2 teaspoons low-fat dairy-free spread
1 medium brown onion (150g),
    chopped finely
4 cups (800g) basmati rice
2 litres (8 cups) chicken stock
1 cup (170g) coarsely chopped raisins
1½ cups loosely packed, coarsely
    chopped fresh coriander

1. Combine chicken, juice, garlic and spices in large bowl, cover; refrigerate 3 hours or overnight.
2. Cook chicken, in batches, on heated lightly oiled grill plate (or grill or barbecue), brushing with a little of the yogurt, until browned all over and cooked through.
3. Meanwhile, heat dairy-free spread in large saucepan; cook onion, stirring, until softened. Add rice; stir to coat in onion mixture. Add stock; bring to a boil. Reduce heat; simmer, covered, stirring occasionally, about 25 minutes or until rice is almost tender. Stir in raisins; cook, covered, 5 minutes.
4. Stir coriander into pilaf off the heat just before serving. Top pilaf with chicken and remaining yogurt.

serves 8

per serving 11.0g fat; 2631kJ

serving suggestion Coleslaw dressed with a red-wine and caraway vinaigrette suits this piquant chicken dish perfectly.

tip Stir some finely chopped and seeded cucumber into the remaining yogurt.

menu suggestion
begin with *char-grilled polenta cakes* page 21
follow with *lime cheesecake* page 96

vegetarian rice paper rolls

preparation time 1 hour • cooking time 15 minutes

Rice stick noodles are available, dried, in both flat and wide or very thin widths; we use the thin, spaghetti-like version in these spring rolls. You need one large bunch of fresh mint and another of fresh coriander for this recipe.

150g rice stick noodles
1 teaspoon sesame oil
1/4 cup (60ml) lime juice
1/4 cup (60ml) sweet chilli sauce
24 x 22cm rice paper sheets
48 large fresh mint leaves
48 fresh coriander sprigs
2 medium carrots (240g),
    grated coarsely
2 medium red capsicums (400g),
    sliced thinly
2 medium yellow capsicums (400g),
    sliced thinly
150g snow peas, sliced thinly
1/4 cup coarsely chopped fresh chives

COCONUT DIPPING SAUCE

1 teaspoon sesame oil
2 cloves garlic, crushed
2 green onions, sliced thickly
2 teaspoons grated fresh ginger
1 1/2 cups (375ml) light coconut milk
1 teaspoon fish sauce

1. Place noodles in large heatproof bowl; cover with boiling water. Stand 5 minutes or until tender; drain. Combine noodles in large bowl with oil, 1 tablespoon of the juice and 2 tablespoons of the chilli sauce (reserve remaining juice and chilli sauce for the coconut dipping sauce).
2. Place one sheet of rice paper in medium bowl of warm water until just softened; carefully lift from water. Place on board; pat dry with absorbent paper. Place 2 mint leaves and 2 coriander sprigs in centre of rice paper; top with some of the carrot, capsicums, snow peas, chives and noodles. Roll to enclose filling, folding in sides after first complete turn of the roll.
3. Repeat with remaining rice paper sheets and vegetable fillings. Serve rolls with coconut dipping sauce.
coconut dipping sauce Heat sesame oil in small saucepan; cook garlic, onion and ginger, stirring, until fragrant. Add coconut milk; simmer, uncovered, about 5 minutes or until mixture thickens slightly. Strain into small bowl. Stir in fish sauce and reserved remaining juice and chilli sauce; cool.

serves 8

per serving 3.7g fat; 481kJ

serving suggestion Serve with stir-fried gai larn (chinese broccoli) in garlic and ginger sauce.

menu suggestion
begin with *chicken wonton soup* page 8
follow with *peach galette* page 107

Lemon grass is easy to grow, especially in tropical regions where lemons do not thrive – hence this tall grass's popularity throughout Southeast Asia.

pumpkin gnocchi

preparation time 50 minutes • cooking time 50 minutes

Gnocchi are small Italian dumplings that can be made from semolina, potato or, as here, pumpkin. While we serve our gnocchi as a vegetarian main course, they also make a good accompaniment to meat or poultry dishes.

16 medium egg tomatoes
(1.2kg), quartered
1.6kg butternut pumpkin
1 egg
2 tablespoons finely chopped
fresh flat-leaf parsley
2 tablespoons finely chopped
fresh basil
2 cups (300g) plain flour
1 cup (150g) self-raising flour
2 teaspoons olive oil
1 small leek (200g), sliced thinly
1.5kg spinach, chopped coarsely
2 tablespoons olive paste
1/2 cup (40g) flaked parmesan cheese

1. Preheat oven to hot.
2. Place tomato in large non-stick baking dish; bake, uncovered, in hot oven about 20 minutes or until browned lightly and softened.
3. Meanwhile, peel pumpkin; chop coarsely. Boil, steam or microwave until tender; drain. Blend or process cooled pumpkin and egg until smooth; place in large bowl. Using hand, mix in herbs and flours. Turn pumpkin dough onto floured surface; knead lightly for about 2 minutes or until smooth. Roll heaped teaspoons of dough into gnocchi-shaped ovals; press lightly against back of fork tines. Place gnocchi on tray. Cover; refrigerate 30 minutes.
4. Heat oil in large non-stick frying pan; cook leek, stirring, until softened. Add spinach; cook, stirring, until spinach is just wilted.
5. Cook gnocchi, uncovered, in large saucepan of boiling water until all gnocchi float to surface. Carefully remove gnocchi from pan, using slotted spoon; drain. Serve gnocchi on spinach-leek mixture; top with tomato, olive paste and cheese.

serves 8
per serving 5.7g fat; 1436kJ

menu suggestion
begin with *low-fat caesar salad* page 16
follow with *crepes and strawberries with caramelised cointreau sauce* page 90

Olive paste is sometimes sold as olive tapenade or olive pâté, and is available, bottled, made from either green or black olives. It makes a good canapé, spread on freshly toasted bread slices.

spinach and cheese quesadillas

preparation time 20 minutes • cooking time 10 minutes

Quesadillas are filled tortillas which are grilled or fried and served with fresh salsa. We used small flour tortillas measuring approximately 16cm in diameter; they are sometimes labelled "fajita tortillas" on the package.

2/3 cup (130g) low-fat cottage cheese
100g spinach leaves, trimmed
1 medium avocado (230g),
  chopped finely
1 cup (200g) canned mexican-style
  beans, drained
125g can corn kernels, drained
2 medium tomatoes (380g), seeded,
  chopped finely
1 small red onion (100g),
  chopped finely
2 medium zucchini (240g),
  grated coarsely
16 small flour tortillas
1 1/2 cups (150g) coarsely grated
  low-fat mozzarella cheese

1. Blend or process cottage cheese and spinach until smooth. Combine avocado, beans, corn, tomato, onion and zucchini in medium bowl.
2. Place eight tortillas on lightly oiled oven tray; divide spinach mixture among tortillas, leaving 2cm border around edge. Divide avocado mixture among tortillas by sprinkling over spinach mixture. Top each with one of the remaining tortillas.
3. Sprinkle mozzarella over quesadilla stacks; place under preheated grill until cheese just melts and browns lightly.

serves 8
per serving 11.2g fat; 1155kJ

menu suggestion
begin with pureed *parsnip and bean soup* page 28
follow with *pear and ginger cake* page 92

Serve quesadillas with a grated cabbage and carrot salad tossed in a lime juice and fresh coriander dressing.

vegetable burgers

preparation time 20 minutes • cooking time 40 minutes

You need to cook ¹/2 cup (100g) long-grain white rice for this recipe.

Life's too short not to eat a burger from time to time, and this one – heavy on flavour yet low in fat – is almost completely devoid of guilt.

1 tablespoon vegetable oil

1 large brown onion (200g), chopped finely

300g button mushrooms, chopped coarsely

1 medium red capsicum (200g), chopped finely

1 clove garlic, crushed

1 cup (200g) red lentils

2 cups (500ml) vegetable stock

1¹/2 cups cooked rice

2 tablespoons finely chopped fresh flat-leaf parsley

¹/3 cup (50g) plain flour

2 medium carrots (240g), grated coarsely

6 small wholemeal bread rolls

225g can sliced beetroot, drained

1¹/2 cups (60g) alfalfa

2 medium tomatoes (380g), sliced thinly

200g low-fat yogurt

1 tablespoon finely chopped fresh mint

1 teaspoon sugar

1. Heat oil in large non-stick frying pan; cook onion, mushrooms, capsicum, garlic and lentils, stirring, until vegetables soften. Add stock; bring to a boil. Reduce heat; simmer, uncovered, stirring occasionally, about 10 minutes or until lentils are tender and stock is absorbed. Remove from heat. Add rice, parsley, flour and half of the carrot; stir to combine.

2. When lentil mixture is cool enough to handle, use hands to shape it into six burger-shaped patties. Cook, in batches, in large heated lightly oiled non-stick frying pan until burgers are browned both sides and heated through.

3. Meanwhile, split bread rolls in half; toast, cut-side up, until browned lightly. Just before serving, sandwich patties with remaining carrot, beetroot, alfalfa, tomato and combined yogurt, mint and sugar in rolls.

serves 6

per serving 6.3g fat; 1568kJ

menu suggestion
begin with *smoked chicken salad* page 14
follow with *melon granita trio* page 104

Oven-roasted potato wedges won't break the fat-count bank when served with these healthy burgers.

risoni with cherry tomatoes, squash and spinach

preparation time 30 minutes • cooking time 30 minutes

You can use any other grain-sized pasta (such as orzo or puntalette) if the risoni is not readily available.

500g cherry tomatoes, halved
500g patty-pan squash, quartered
8 cloves garlic, quartered
1/4 cup firmly packed fresh oregano
1/4 cup (60ml) olive oil
1/3 cup (50g) pine nuts
1kg risoni
3 red thai chillies, seeded,
   chopped finely
250g baby spinach, trimmed
1/2 cup firmly packed, coarsely
   chopped fresh basil

1. Preheat oven to moderate.
2. Combine tomato, squash, garlic, half of the oregano and 1 tablespoon of the oil in large shallow non-stick baking dish. Roast, uncovered, in moderate oven 20 minutes. Add pine nuts to vegetable mixture; roast, uncovered, about 10 minutes or until tomato is tender and nuts are browned.
3. Meanwhile, cook pasta, uncovered, in large saucepan of boiling water until just tender; drain. Cover to keep warm.
4. Heat remaining oil in large saucepan; cook chilli, stirring, 1 minute. Stir in pasta, spinach, basil and remaining oregano; toss gently until combined. Stir in tomato mixture; serve immediately.

serves 8

per serving 13.0g fat; 2353kJ

serving suggestion Warmed crusty bread rolls, such as rosette, are all you need with this main course.

menu suggestion
begin with *steamed sweet chilli prawn dumplings* page 23
follow with *chocolate fudge cake* page 99

mixed mushroom ragout with soft polenta

preparation time 20 minutes • cooking time 50 minutes

2 tablespoons low-fat
   dairy-free spread
2 large brown onions (400g),
   chopped coarsely
3 cloves garlic, crushed
1/4 cup (35g) plain flour
400g button mushrooms
400g swiss brown
   mushrooms, quartered
400g flat mushrooms, sliced thickly
2 tablespoons tomato paste
2/3 cup (160ml) dry red wine
1.25 litres (5 cups) water
1 litre (4 cups) vegetable stock
2 teaspoons finely chopped
   fresh thyme
2 cups (340g) polenta
1 cup (250ml) skim milk
1/4 cup (20g) finely grated
   parmesan cheese

1. Heat dairy-free spread in large saucepan; cook onion and garlic, stirring, until onion softens. Add flour; cook, stirring, until mixture bubbles. Add mushrooms; cook, stirring, until mushrooms are just tender.
2. Add tomato paste and wine to mushroom mixture; bring to a boil. Reduce heat; simmer, uncovered, until liquid reduces by half. Add 2 cups of the water and half of the stock; return to a boil. Reduce heat; simmer, uncovered, 30 minutes. Stir in thyme.
3. Meanwhile, combine the remaining water and remaining stock in another large saucepan; bring to a boil. Add polenta; cook, stirring, until polenta boils and thickens. Add milk and cheese; cook, stirring, until cheese has melted.
4. Serve mushroom ragout on polenta.

serves 8

per serving 4.7g fat; 1084kJ

serving suggestion Top with sprigs of fresh thyme.

menu suggestion
begin with *tomato tarte tatin* page 30
follow with *grilled figs with cinnamon-scented ricotta* page 93

crepes and strawberries with caramelised cointreau sauce

preparation time 15 minutes (plus standing time) • cooking time 30 minutes

Cointreau is a colourless orange-flavoured liqueur. You can replace it with Grand Marnier, Triple-Sec or brandy.

3/4 cup (110g) plain flour
1/2 cup (110g) sugar
1 egg, beaten lightly
1 1/3 cups (330ml) skim milk
1 teaspoon vegetable oil
1/4 lime
1 teaspoon low-fat dairy-free spread
2 tablespoons Cointreau
1/4 cup (60ml) water
500g strawberries, halved

1. Combine flour and 1 tablespoon of the sugar in medium bowl. Gradually whisk in combined egg, milk and oil until mixture is smooth; strain batter into large jug. Cover; refrigerate for 30 minutes.
2. Meanwhile, push fork into skin-side of lime. Melt dairy-free spread in large frying pan; cook remaining sugar, stirring with lime wedge, until sugar caramelises. Remove from heat; stir in liqueur and the water. Return to heat; bring to a boil. Reduce heat; simmer, uncovered, until mixture reduces by half. Add strawberries; stir gently until well coated then remove from heat.
3. Pour 2 tablespoons of batter into small heated lightly greased non-stick frying pan; cook crepe until browned lightly both sides. Repeat with remaining batter to make 12 crepes.
4. Serve crepes warm, filled with strawberries in sauce.

serves 6

per serving 2.4g fat; 975kJ

tip Stirring the sugar with lime wedge gives a slight lime flavour to the sauce. Orange juice can be substituted for Cointreau for a non-alcoholic alternative.

Serve the crepes garnished with lime wedges and shredded fresh mint leaves.

desserts

pear and ginger cake

preparation time 15 minutes • cooking time 45 minutes (plus standing time)

You need eight even-sized pear halves for this recipe; arrange them on cake mixture before baking in such a way that each serving will includes a whole pear half. This cake is best served warm.

1 cup (150g) self-raising flour
1/2 cup (75g) plain flour
1 tablespoon ground ginger
1/4 teaspoon bicarbonate of soda
1/3 cup (120g) treacle
60g low-fat dairy-free spread
2/3 cup (150g) firmly packed
   brown sugar
1 egg, beaten lightly
1/4 cup (60ml) milk
825g can pear halves, drained
1/4 cup (80g) apricot jam

1. Preheat oven to moderate. Lightly grease 20cm x 30cm lamington pan; line base with baking paper.
2. Sift flours with ginger and soda into large bowl.
3. Combine treacle, dairy-free spread and sugar in small saucepan; stir over heat, without boiling, until sugar dissolves. Cool 5 minutes.
4. Pour treacle mixture into flour mixture; stir until combined. Stir in egg and milk.
5. Pour cake mixture into prepared pan; top with pear, cut-side down, arranged to make eight equal-sized servings. Bake in moderate oven about 40 minutes; stand cake in pan 10 minutes. Turn onto wire rack; remove baking paper. Turn cake top-side up to cool.
6. Warm jam in small saucepan over low heat. Strain jam through sieve; brush warm cake with warm jam.

serves 8

per serving 4.1g fat; 1286kJ

serving suggestion Serve with a jug of low-fat custard.

grilled figs with cinnamon-scented ricotta

preparation time 10 minutes • cooking time 5 minutes

9 large figs (720g), halved
1/4 cup (60ml) lime juice
1/4 cup (50g) firmly packed
   brown sugar
1 cup (200g) low-fat ricotta cheese
1/2 teaspoon ground cinnamon
1 tablespoon caster sugar

1. Place figs, cut-side up, on large oven tray; brush with combined juice and brown sugar. Place under heated grill until figs are browned lightly.
2. Meanwhile, combine cheese, cinnamon and caster sugar in small bowl. Serve ricotta mixture with figs.

serves 6

per serving 3.3g fat; 568kJ

serving suggestion An accompanying glass of chilled Sauternes makes this a dessert to die for!

Ricotta means re-cooked in Italian – a reference to the fact that it's made from the whey from a stretched-curd cheese such as mozzarella or provolone. In this recipe, it provides a creamy yet low-fat accompaniment for the figs.

black forest parfaits

preparation time 30 minutes (plus refrigeration time)

We used Flyte chocolate bars for this recipe, which are low-fat, bite-sized milk chocolate bars with a light whipped chocolate centre. Jam rollettes are miniature Swiss rolls.

2 x 85g packets cherry jelly crystals
6 jam rollettes (150g),
 chopped coarsely
1/4 cup (60ml) sweet sherry
425g can stoneless black
 cherries, drained
1 1/2 cups (375ml) low-fat
 vanilla custard
3 x 20g low-fat chocolate bars,
 sliced thinly

1. Make jelly according to directions on packet; place in large jug. Refrigerate about 1 hour or until jelly is almost set.
2. Meanwhile, combine rollettes and sherry in small bowl. Reserve half of the rollette mixture; cover until required. Divide remaining half among six 1 1/3-cup (330ml) serving glasses.
3. Pour half of the jelly mixture evenly over rollette mixture in glasses; sprinkle with half of the cherries. Refrigerate 5 minutes. Continue layering with remaining rollette mixture, then all of the custard, the remaining jelly and, finally, the remaining cherries. Cover parfaits; refrigerate overnight.
4. Serve parfaits sprinkled evenly with chocolate.

serves 6

per serving 3.2g fat; 1277kJ

serving suggestion Serve topped with whipped light cream.

banana pudding with espresso syrup

preparation time 15 minutes • cooking time 50 minutes

You will need 4 large overripe bananas for this recipe.

2 eggs
1 cup (200g) firmly packed
   brown sugar
2 cups mashed banana
1/2 cup (140g) low-fat yogurt
40g butter, melted
2 teaspoons vanilla essence
2 cups (300g) self-raising flour
1 1/2 teaspoons ground cinnamon
1 teaspoon bicarbonate of soda

ESPRESSO SYRUP
3/4 cup (165g) sugar
3/4 cup (180ml) water
1 tablespoon dry instant coffee

1. Preheat oven to moderate. Lightly grease deep 20cm-round cake pan; line base with baking paper.
2. Beat eggs in small bowl with electric mixer until thick and creamy. Add sugar; continue beating 5 minutes.
3. Fold in banana, yogurt, butter and essence, then sifted flour, cinnamon and soda; pour mixture into prepared pan. Bake in moderate oven about 50 minutes. Stand cake in pan for 5 minutes. Turn onto wire rack over tray; remove paper. Drizzle half of the hot espresso syrup over hot cake; serve immediately with remaining half of hot espresso syrup in heatproof jug.

espresso syrup Combine sugar, the water and coffee in small saucepan; stir over heat, without boiling, until sugar dissolves. Bring to a boil; transfer to heatproof jug.

serves 8

per serving 6.1g fat; 1934kJ

serving suggestion Serve hot pudding with low-fat vanilla ice-cream.

lime cheesecake

preparation time 30 minutes (plus refrigeration time) • cooking time 10 minutes

The long refrigeration times required for this cheesecake are a bonus when entertaining… make it ahead so you're free to devote all your attention to the rest of the menu on the day of the meal.

80g plain biscuits
40g low-fat dairy-free spread, melted
2 teaspoons gelatine
1 tablespoon water
1/3 cup (80ml) lime juice
2/3 cup (150g) sugar
1/2 cup (100g) low-fat ricotta cheese
100g packaged low-fat cream cheese
2 teaspoons finely grated lime rind
3 egg whites

1. Grease 18cm springform pan; line base with baking paper.
2. Blend or process biscuits and dairy-free spread until mixture resembles fine breadcrumbs. Using one hand, press biscuit mixture evenly over base of prepared pan. Refrigerate until firm.
3. Sprinkle gelatine over the water in heatproof jug; stand jug in medium saucepan of simmering water. Stir until gelatine dissolves; reserve mixture.
4. Combine juice and sugar in small saucepan. Stir over heat, without boiling, until sugar dissolves; bring to a boil. Reduce heat; simmer 1 minute.
5. Meanwhile, beat cheeses and rind in medium bowl with electric mixer until mixture is smooth.
6. Beat egg whites in small bowl with electric mixer until soft peaks form; with motor operating, gradually add hot sugar syrup. Whisk slightly warm gelatine mixture and egg white mixture into cheese mixture; pour mixture into prepared pan. Cover; refrigerate about 2 hours or until set.

serves 8

per serving 6.7g fat; 773kJ

serving suggestion Pipe whipped light cream on cheesecake and decorate with thin lime wedges just before serving.

If you don't own a citrus zester, grate only the green outer rind of a lime on the tiniest holes of a four-sided grater. Avoid grating any of the bitter white pith.

chocolate mousse

preparation time 10 minutes (plus refrigeration time)

The word mousse is a French description for froth or foam, a look usually achieved by lots of kilojoule-laden whipped cream. Here, we've used low-fat Frûche for equally delicious results, but without the excess fat and energy.

1 tablespoon dry instant coffee
1 tablespoon cocoa powder
2 teaspoons hot water
160g dark chocolate, melted
3 cups (800g) french vanilla
　low-fat Frûche
50g dark chocolate, grated, extra

1. Dissolve coffee and cocoa in the water in medium bowl. Stir in melted chocolate and Frûche; beat with electric mixer on medium speed about 3 minutes or until mixture is smooth.
2. Divide mixture evenly among eight $1/2$-cup (125ml) serving glasses. Cover; refrigerate overnight.
3. Serve chocolate mousse sprinkled with extra chocolate.

serves 8

per serving 8.09g fat; 955kJ

tip Frûche is a commercial dessert having less than 0.5g fat per 100g; substitute fromage frais or a low-fat vanilla yogurt if you cannot find it but be aware that the fat count will rise slightly if Frûche isn't used.

serving suggestion Serve mousse topped with fresh berries – raspberries team especially well with chocolate.

chocolate fudge cake

preparation time 20 minutes • cooking time 40 minutes

You'll never believe that you can indulge in chocolate-lover's heaven with a fudgey sensation like this without having to worry about the fat and kilojoule count.

85g dark chocolate, chopped finely
1/2 cup (50g) cocoa powder
1 cup (200g) firmly packed
   brown sugar
1/2 cup (125ml) boiling water
2 egg yolks
1/4 cup (30g) almond meal
1/3 cup (50g) wholemeal plain flour
4 egg whites

1. Preheat oven to moderate. Line base and side of deep 20cm-round cake pan.
2. Combine chocolate, cocoa and sugar with the water in large bowl; stir until smooth. Add egg yolks; whisk to combine. Fold in almond meal and flour.
3. Beat egg whites in small bowl with electric mixer until firm peaks form. Gently fold egg white mixture into chocolate mixture, in two batches; pour into prepared pan.
4. Bake in moderate oven about 40 minutes. Stand in pan 5 minutes. Turn onto wire rack; remove paper.

serves 8

per serving 7.5g fat; 958kJ

serving suggestion Serve cake warm, dusted with icing sugar and dotted with fresh strawberries.

poached nashi in asian-spiced syrup

preparation time 5 minutes • cooking time 40 minutes

The word nashi is Japanese for pear, and in fact this crisp, juicy pale-green fruit is often called the Japanese or Asian pear even though it is quite similar to an apple in appearance and a quince in versatility.

6 medium nashi (1.2kg)
2 cups (440g) sugar
1 litre (4 cups) water
1 vanilla bean
2 cinnamon sticks
2 star anise
2 cardamom pods, bruised

1. Peel nashi, leaving stems intact.
2. Combine sugar with the water in large saucepan; stir over heat, without boiling, until sugar dissolves.
3. Split vanilla bean in half lengthways; scrape seeds directly into sugar syrup. Add nashi to syrup with cinnamon, star anise and cardamom; bring to a boil. Reduce heat; simmer, covered, about 20 minutes or until nashi are just tender, turning occasionally. Remove from heat; cool in syrup.
4. Remove nashi from syrup. Strain syrup over medium jug; discard solids and all but 2 cups of the syrup.
5. Bring reserved syrup to a boil in small saucepan. Reduce heat; simmer, uncovered, about 15 minutes or until syrup reduces by half. Remove from heat; cool. Divide nashi among serving bowls; drizzle with syrup.

serves 6

per serving 0.2g fat; 1472kJ

serving suggestion Serve with whipped light cream or low-fat fruit yogurt.

rhubarb and strawberry sponge pudding

preparation time 20 minutes • cooking time 50 minutes

Actually a vegetable, rhubarb is a member of the buckwheat family. It has an intensely tart flavour which makes it a natural dessert and pie filling when sweetened and combined with other fruit. You will need about 10 stems of rhubarb to make this recipe.

5 cups (700g) coarsely chopped, trimmed rhubarb
2 tablespoons sugar
2 tablespoons orange juice
500g strawberries, hulled, sliced thinly
280g packet sponge cake mix

1. Preheat oven to moderate.
2. Combine rhubarb, sugar and juice in large saucepan; cook over low heat, stirring, until sugar dissolves. Cook, uncovered, further 10 minutes or until rhubarb is tender. Stir in strawberries. Divide among eight 1-cup (250ml) ovenproof dishes; bake, uncovered, in moderate oven 5 minutes.
3. Meanwhile, prepare sponge according to instructions on packet. Top rhubarb mixture evenly with sponge mixture; bake, uncovered, in moderate oven about 30 minutes.

serves 8

per serving 1.6g fat; 267kJ

serving suggestion Serve with low-fat custard or thickened light cream.

pink grapefruit souffles

preparation time 30 minutes • cooking time 25 minutes

Grenadine is a deep-red syrup based on pomegranate juice and used to both colour and sweeten desserts and drinks. Originally made entirely from pomegranates grown on Grenada, a Caribbean island, nowadays it is based on pomegranates from any source and can contain the juice from other fruits as well. Some versions of grenadine contain alcohol; the one we used did not.

$^{1}/_{3}$ cup (75g) caster sugar
$^{1}/_{3}$ cup (50g) plain flour
$^{3}/_{4}$ cup (180ml) skim milk
1 tablespoon finely grated
    pink grapefruit rind
$^{1}/_{4}$ cup (60ml) pink grapefruit juice
1 teaspoon grenadine
40g low-fat dairy-free spread
3 egg yolks
5 egg whites

1. Preheat oven to hot.
2. Lightly grease six $^{3}/_{4}$-cup (180ml) ovenproof dishes. Sprinkle bases and sides of dishes with a little of the sugar.
3. Combine remaining sugar with flour in medium saucepan; gradually whisk in milk. Cook, stirring, until mixture boils and thickens. Whisk in rind, juice, grenadine and dairy-free spread; remove from heat.
4. Transfer mixture to large bowl. Whisk in egg yolks, one at a time.
5. Beat egg whites in small bowl with electric mixer until soft peaks form. Fold a quarter of the egg white mixture into grapefruit mixture; fold in remaining egg white mixture. Spoon into prepared dishes on oven tray; cook, uncovered, in hot oven about 15 minutes or until tops are brown.

serves 6

per serving 5.6g fat; 672kJ

tip You can also find a pomegranate syrup in Middle-Eastern food shops which can be substituted for the grenadine. It has a much tarter flavour, however, would work well with the grapefruit in this recipe. Alternatively, you could use raspberry cordial or topping instead of the grenadine to enhance the pink colour.

serving suggestion Serve dusted with icing sugar.

Grapefruit probably got their name because they grow in clusters, looking like an oversized bunch of grapes. Pink or ruby grapefruit have coral-pink flesh and shell-pink skin, and are sweeter and juicier than the yellow-skinned variety.

melon granita trio

preparation time 45 minutes (plus freezing time) • cooking time 10 minutes

You need a small rockmelon (1.3kg), a small honeydew (1.3kg), and a small watermelon (1.5kg) for this recipe.

3 cups (750ml) water
1¹⁄₂ cups (330g) sugar
800g seeded, peeled, coarsely chopped rockmelon
800g seeded, peeled, coarsely chopped honeydew melon
800g seeded, peeled, coarsely chopped watermelon

1. Combine the water and sugar in medium saucepan. Stir over heat, without boiling, until sugar dissolves; bring to a boil. Reduce heat; simmer, uncovered, without stirring, about 2 minutes or until syrup thickens slightly.
2. Blend or process rockmelon until almost smooth; push through sieve into shallow metal cake pan. Combine with a third of the sugar syrup. Repeat process with honeydew and half of the remaining syrup in separate metal cake pan, then with watermelon and remaining syrup in another cake pan.
3. Cover each pan with aluminium foil; freeze about 3 hours or until granita mixtures are just set.
4. Keeping granita mixtures separate, scrape into bowls, then beat each with electric mixer until smooth. Return each to their respective pans, cover with foil; freeze overnight or until each granita sets firmly.
5. Serve granita, layered in alternate scoops, in individual glasses.

serves 8

per serving 0.6g fat; 979kJ

serving suggestion Granitas are delicious on a hot day served on top of bowls of seasonal fruit salad.

honey buttermilk ice-cream with fresh fruit salsa

preparation time 30 minutes (plus freezing time) • cooking time 15 minutes

2 teaspoons gelatine
1/4 cup (60ml) water
1 1/2 cups (375ml) low-fat
   evaporated milk
1/2 cup (175g) honey
1 1/2 cups (375ml) buttermilk

FRUIT SALSA
1 small pineapple (800g),
   chopped coarsely
1 large mango (600g),
   chopped coarsely
3 medium kiwi fruit (255g),
   chopped coarsely
250g strawberries, chopped coarsely

1. Sprinkle gelatine over the water in small heatproof jug; stand jug in pan of simmering water. Stir until gelatine dissolves; cool.
2. Meanwhile, place evaporated milk in medium saucepan; bring to a boil. Remove from heat; stir in gelatine mixture and honey. Transfer to medium bowl; cool.
3. Beat buttermilk in small bowl with electric mixer until buttermilk is frothy.
4. Beat evaporated milk mixture with electric mixer until light and frothy. With motor operating, gradually pour in buttermilk; beat until combined.
5. Pour into 2-litre (8 cup) metal container. Cover with aluminium foil; freeze about 3 hours or until just set.
6. Beat ice-cream with electric mixer until smooth. Re-cover with foil; freeze overnight or until set. Serve ice-cream with fruit salsa.
fruit salsa Combine fruit in medium bowl.

serves 6 (approximately 2 litres ice-cream)
per serving 7g fat; 1426kJ
tip Ice-cream can also be made in an ice-cream maker.

Buttermilk is a tangy dairy product made in a similar way to yogurt. It has a fat content of 1.8g per 100ml. We used low-fat evaporated milk with a fat count of 1.6g per 100ml.

guilt-free tiramisu

preparation time 20 minutes (plus refrigeration time)

Tiramisu, translated roughly as "pick-me-up", is usually made of savoiardi (sponge-finger biscuits) soaked in coffee and marsala, then layered with masses of mascarpone and topped with cream. Our version is no less delicious… but far, far less laden with fat!

1 tablespoon dry instant coffee
3/4 cup (180ml) boiling water
2 tablespoons marsala
125g packet sponge-finger biscuits
1 cup (200g) low-fat ricotta
1/2 cup (120g) light sour cream
2 tablespoons caster sugar
2 teaspoons cocoa powder

1. Dissolve coffee in the boiling water in medium bowl; stir in marsala. Set aside 18 biscuits; coarsely chop remaining biscuits.
2. Stand three biscuits upright in each of six 3/4-cup (180ml) glasses; drizzle biscuits with half of the coffee mixture.
3. Beat ricotta, cream and sugar with electric mixer in small bowl for about 4 minutes or until mixture just thickens slightly. Divide half of the ricotta mixture among glasses; sprinkle with chopped biscuits. Drizzle with remaining coffee mixture; top with remaining ricotta mixture.
4. Dust each tiramisu with sifted cocoa. Cover; refrigerate 3 hours or overnight before serving.

serves 6

per serving 7.8g fat; 757kJ

serving suggestion Stirring about 1/2 cup pureed fresh strawberries or mango into the ricotta mixture is a nice addition to this dessert … and, of course, accompany it with tiny cups of good espresso.

peach galette

preparation time 10 minutes • cooking time 15 minutes

A galette is a French flaky pastry tart that can be either savoury or sweet, and makes a popular summer dessert. Any of the season's stone fruits, such as plums or nectarines, can be substituted for the peaches.

1 sheet ready-rolled puff pastry with
 canola, thawed
3 medium peaches (450g)
1 tablespoon brown sugar
1 tablespoon plum jam,
 warmed, strained

1. Preheat oven to hot. Place pastry sheet on lightly greased oven tray.
2. Place unpeeled peaches in large heat-proof bowl; cover with boiling water. Stand about 1 minute or until skins can be slipped off peaches easily. Slice peaches thinly; discard seeds.
3. Arrange peach slices on pastry, leaving 2cm border around edge; fold over edges of pastry. Sprinkle sugar evenly over peach galette.
4. Bake galette in hot oven about 15 minutes or until pastry is browned lightly. Brush hot galette with jam.

serves 6

per serving 6.4g fat; 602kJ

serving suggestion Serve sprinkled with icing sugar.

mini lemon yogurt cakes with syrup

preparation time 10 minutes • cooking time 15 minutes

The combination of lemon, yogurt and poppy seeds lends an eastern Mediterranean accent to these morsels.

1/3 cup (50g) self-raising flour
1/4 cup (55g) caster sugar
1 1/2 tablespoons cornflour
1/4 teaspoon bicarbonate of soda
1 teaspoon poppy seeds
1 egg yolk
1/4 cup (70g) yogurt
1/2 teaspoon finely grated lemon rind
1 teaspoon lemon juice
10g butter, melted

LEMON SYRUP
1 medium lemon (140g)
1/4 cup (55g) sugar
1/4 cup (60ml) water

1. Preheat oven to moderate.
2. Sift flour, sugar, cornflour and soda into small bowl; stir in seeds, yolk, yogurt, rind, juice and butter.
3. Drop rounded teaspoons of mixture into baby patty cases on oven tray. Bake in moderate oven 10 minutes. Drizzle or brush hot lemon syrup over hot cakes.
lemon syrup Using vegetable peeler, remove rind from lemon; shred peel finely. Juice the peeled lemon; place 2 teaspoons of the juice (reserve remainder for another use) in small saucepan with shredded rind, sugar and the water. Stir over heat, without boiling, until sugar dissolves. Boil, uncovered, without stirring, about 5 minutes or until mixture thickens slightly; transfer to small heatproof jug.

makes 30

per cake 0.6g fat; 121kJ

Use a vegetable peeler to remove the lemon rind before you juice the citrus.

treats

rum balls

preparation time 15 minutes (plus refrigeration time)

*The trick is to stick to just taking one...
well then, maybe two.*

4 cups (400g) cake crumbs
1/4 cup (25g) cocoa powder
1/4 cup (80g) apricot jam, warmed
2 tablespoons dark rum
2 tablespoons water
2/3 cup (70g) chocolate sprinkles

1. Combine cake crumbs and sifted
cocoa in large bowl. Add jam, rum
and the water; stir until mixture
comes together.
2. Roll rounded teaspoons of the
mixture into balls. Roll balls in sprinkles;
place on tray. Cover; refrigerate 2 hours
before serving.

makes 50 balls

per ball 1.5g fat; 173kJ

serving suggestion For a flavour
variation, the rum and water can be
replaced with 1/3 cup Cointreau for an
orange twist, or 1/3 cup Malibu for a
coconut flavour.

minted meringue sticks

preparation time 10 minute • cooking time 40 minutes

The satisfying crunch of crisp meringue combines with the sensuous delight of chocolate for a more-ish indulgence that's practically guilt-free.

2 egg whites
1/2 cup (110g) caster sugar
1/4 teaspoon peppermint essence
40g dark chocolate Melts, melted

1. Preheat oven to slow.
2. Beat egg whites in small bowl with electric mixer until soft peaks form. Gradually add sugar, 1 tablespoon at a time, beating well after each addition, until all sugar has been added and dissolved. Fold essence gently into meringue mixture.
3. Grease two oven trays; line with baking paper. Place meringue mixture into piping bag fitted with 1.5cm plain tube; pipe 12cm logs onto prepared trays. Bake in slow oven about 40 minutes or until crisp and dry. Cool meringues on trays.
4. Drizzle or pipe meringue sticks with melted chocolate.

makes 24

per stick 0.5g fat; 114kJ

tip One of the best ways to melt chocolate is in an uncovered microwave-safe container (not one made from plastic because it's not a good heat conductor) on HIGH in 30-second bursts.

sugared fruit jellies

preparation time 15 minutes (plus standing and refrigeration time) • cooking time 15 minutes

To make decoratively shaped jellies, you can pour the mixture into lightly oiled individual moulds, or use a small pastry cutter to make shapes from the set jelly.

2 x 85g packets strawberry
   jelly crystals
1 tablespoon gelatine
1 cup (250ml) boiling water
2 tablespoons glucose syrup
1¹/₂ cups (330g) caster sugar

1. Combine jelly crystals, gelatine and the water in small bowl, stirring until crystals are dissolved. Cover; refrigerate overnight.
2. Transfer mixture to medium saucepan. Add glucose and 1 cup (220g) of the sugar. Stir over heat, without boiling, until sugar dissolves; bring to a boil. Reduce heat; simmer, uncovered, skimming occasionally, 10 minutes.
3. Pour mixture into lightly oiled 8cm x 26cm bar pan; stand 15 minutes. Cover; refrigerate overnight.
4. To remove jelly from pan, run small wet knife around inside of pan; turn jelly out onto sheet of baking paper. Cut jelly evenly into four strips lengthways; cut each strip into 13 cubes. Coat jelly cubes evenly with remaining sugar.

makes 52

per jelly 0g fat; 167kJ

tip Use lime or orange jelly for alternative colours and flavours.

hazelnut biscotti

preparation time 10 minutes • cooking time 45 minutes

Biscotti, Italian in origin, owe their crispness to the fact that they are baked twice. Their delicate flavor well suits fruit ices, and they're great for dunking in a glass of espresso.

1¹/₃ cups (200g) plain flour
¹/₃ cup (50g) self-raising flour
1 cup (220g) caster sugar
2 eggs, beaten lightly
¹/₂ cup (75g) roasted hazelnuts
1 teaspoon vanilla essence

1. Preheat oven to moderate.
2. Sift flours and sugar into large bowl. Add egg, nuts and essence; stir until mixture becomes a firm dough. Knead on lightly floured surface board until mixture just comes together; shape mixture into 25cm log. Place on greased oven tray; bake, in moderate oven about 35 minutes or until firm; cool on tray.
4. Using serrated or electric knife, cut log into 5mm diagonal slices. Place slices on ungreased oven trays; bake in moderate oven about 10 minutes or until biscotti are dry and crisp.

makes 25 slices

per slice 2.4g fat; 389kJ

tip To roast hazelnuts, spread nuts on oven tray; roast in moderate oven about 5 minutes or until nuts are golden brown (stir nuts once during toasting). Wrap nuts in tea-towel; rub vigorously to remove most of the skin.

sugared pastry twists

preparation time 5 minutes • cooking time 15 minutes

1 sheet ready-rolled puff pastry, thawed
1 egg white
3 teaspoons caster sugar
1/2 teaspoon ground cinnamon

1. Preheat oven to moderate.
2. Brush pastry with egg white; sprinkle evenly with combined sugar and cinnamon.
3. Using a fluted pastry wheel, cut pastry sheet in half. Cut each half crossways into 5mm strips.
4. Twist each pastry strip; place on lightly greased oven tray. Bake in moderate oven about 15 minutes or until pastry browns lightly.

makes 96

per serving 0.4g fat; 30kJ

ALMOND

flaked paper-thin slices.

meal also known as finely ground almonds; powdered to a flour-like texture, used in baking or as a thickening agent.

slivered small lengthways-cut pieces.

BAKING POWDER a raising agent consisting mainly of 2 parts cream of tartar to 1 part bicarbonate of soda (baking soda).

BASIL a member of the mint family (Ocimum spp), basil is an aromatic herb with both culinary and medicinal uses. Varieties include opal basil (purple leaves), lemon basil and cinnamon basil.

sweet basil or common basil has a strong smell similar to cloves or licorice and is an essential ingredient in many Italian dishes as it goes well with tomatoes. Available in most greengrocers and supermarkets; use the leaves only, discarding the stems.

thai also known as bai kaprow or holy basil, Thai basil has small, crinkly leaves with a strong, somewhat bitter, licorice flavour. Most often used in stir-fries.

BEEF

eye fillet tenderloin.

mince also known as ground beef.

rib-eye available as steak and whole piece for roasting. A tender cut also known as scotch fillet.

rump steak boneless tender cut

BEETROOT also known as beets. Baby beetroot leaves, small seedling leaves, are sold as a salad vegetable. Leaves of the adult plant can also be cooked as a vegetable.

BICARBONATE OF SODA also known as baking soda.

BOK CHOY also called pak choi or Chinese white cabbage; has a fresh, mild mustard taste and is good braised or in stir-fries. Baby bok choy is also available.

BREADCRUMBS

packaged fine-textured, crunchy, purchased, white breadcrumbs.

stale 1- or 2-day-old bread made into crumbs by grating, blending or processing.

BURGHUL also known as bulghur wheat; hulled steamed wheat kernels that, once dried are crushed into various size grains. Used in Middle-Eastern dishes such as kibbeh and tabbouleh.

BEANS throughout this book, we used the canned small white beans (phaseolus vulgaris) of which there are many kinds similar in appearance and flavour to one another: cannellini. great northern, navy and haricot beans. Sometimes canned varieties are labelled "butter" beans but in fact butter beans are more floury, larger and kidney-shaped.

CAPERBERRIES fruit formed after buds on a caper bush have flowered; caperberries are sold pickled in brine.

CAPERS the grey-green buds of a warm climate (usually Mediterranean) shrub sold either dried and salted or pickled in a vinegar brine; used to enhance sauces and dressings with their piquant flavour.

CAYENNE PEPPER a thin-fleshed, long, extremely hot red chilli; often purchased dried and ground.

CHEESE

cheddar The most widely eaten cheese in the world, cheddar is a semi-hard cow milk cheese originally made in England. We used a low-fat variety with a fat content of not more than 7%.

fetta A salty white cheese with milky, fresh acidity, fetta is one of the cornerstones of the Greek kitchen. Most commonly made from cow milk, though sheep and goat milk varieties are available; we used a low-fat fetta with an average fat content of 15%.

parmesan Also known as parmigiano, parmesan is a hard, grainy cow milk cheese, originating in the Parma region of Italy. Mainly grated as a topping for pasta, soups and other savoury dishes, it is also delicious eaten with fruit.

ricotta a low-fat, fresh unripened cheese made from whey with 8.5% fat.

CHICKEN

breast fillet breast halved, skinned and boned.

mince also known as ground chicken

tenderloin thin strip of meat lying just under the breast.

thigh fillet thigh with skin and centre bone intact; sometimes known as a chicken chop.

CHINESE BROCCOLI vegetable also known as gai larn.

CHINESE CABBAGE also known as Peking cabbage or wong bok.

CHOY SUM also known as flowering bok choy or flowering white cabbage.

CIABATTA in Italian, the word means 'slipper', which is the traditional shape of this popular crisp-crusted white wood-fired bread.

COCONUT MILK we used a canned light coconut milk with a fat content of less than 6%.

COOKING-OIL SPRAY we used a cholesterol-free cooking spray made from canola oil.

CORNFLOUR also known as cornstarch; used as a thickening agent in cooking.

CORNMEAL ground dried corn (maize); available in different textures, the coarse one of which is known as polenta.

COS LETTUCE also known as romaine and is the traditional caesar salad lettuce; has crisp, elongated leaves.

COUSCOUS a fine, grain-like cereal product, originally from North Africa; made from semolina.

CURRY POWDER a blend of spices, as individual as the maker, although most curry powders do contain ground chilli, cumin, coriander, turmeric and cardamom in varying proportions.

ESSENCES also known as extracts; generally the by-product of distillation of plants. We used peppermint essence and vanilla essence in this book.

FIVE-SPICE POWDER a fragrant mixture of ground cinnamon, cloves, star-anise, Sichuan pepper and fennel seeds.

FLOUR

plain an all-purpose flour, made from wheat.

self-raising plain flour combined with baking powder in the proportion of 1 cup flour to 2 teaspoons baking powder.

GARAM MASALA a blend of spices, originating in North India; based on varying proportions of cardamom, cinnamon, cloves, coriander, fennel and cumin, roasted and ground together.

GINGER, FRESH also known as green or root ginger; the thick gnarled root of a tropical plant.

Can be kept, peeled, covered with dry sherry in a jar and refrigerated, or frozen in an airtight container.

HARISSA a fiery Moroccan blend of caraway, cumin, chill, garlic and various other spices processed with oil into a paste; used as an ingredient in cooking and as a condiment at the table.

HAZELNUT MEAL also known as ground hazelnuts; powdered to a flour-like texture, used in baking or as a thickening agent.

KAFFIR LIME

fruit medium-sized citrus fruit with wrinkly yellow-green skin, used in Thai cooking.

leaves aromatic leaves used fresh or dried in Asian dishes.

KUMARA Polynesian name of orange-fleshed sweet potato often confused with yam.

LAMB

cutlet small, tender rib chop.

fillet tenderloin; the smaller piece of meat from a row of loin chops or cutlets.

LEMON GRASS a tall, clumping, lemon- smelling and tasting, sharp-edged grass; the white lower part of each stem is chopped and used in Asian cooking or for tea.

LOW-FAT CUSTARD we used trim custard with 0.9% fat.

LOW-FAT DAIRY-FREE SPREAD we used a polyunsaturated, cholesterol-free, reduced-fat diet spread made of vegetable oils, water and gelatine having 2.35g of fat per 5g.

LOW-FAT ICE CREAM we used an ice-cream with 3% fat.

LOW-FAT MAYONNAISE we used cholesterol-free mayonnaise with 3% fat.

LOW-FAT SOUR CREAM we used light sour cream with 18.5% fat.

LOW-FAT THICKENED CREAM we used thickened cream with 18% fat.

LOW-FAT YOGURT we used yogurt with a fat content of less than 0.2%.

MELONS

rockmelon oval melon with orange flesh also known as a cantaloupe.

watermelon large green-skinned melon with crisp, juicy, deep pink flesh.

honeydew an oval melon with delicate taste and pale green flesh.

MESCLUN mixed baby salad leaves also sold as salad mix or gourmet salad mix; a mixture of assorted young lettuce and other green leaves.

MEXICAN-STYLE BEANS a canned mixture of either haricot or pinto beans cooked with tomato, peppers, onion, garlic and various spices.

MILK

buttermilk sold alongside fresh milk products in supermarkets; despite the implication of its name, is low in fat. Commercially made, by a method similar to yogurt. A good low-fat substitute for dairy products such as cream or sour cream; good in baking and in salad dressings.

skim we used milk with 0.15% fat content or lower.

MINCE MEAT also known as ground meat.

MIRIN a sweet low-alcohol rice wine used in Japanese cooking; sometimes referred to simply as rice wine but should not be confused with sake, the Japanese rice wine made for drinking.

MUSHROOMS

button small, cultivated white mushrooms having a delicate, subtle flavour.

flat large, flat mushrooms with a rich earthy flavour, ideal for filling and barbecuing. They are sometimes misnamed field mushrooms which are wild mushrooms.

MUSTARD

dijon a pale brown, distinctively flavoured, fairly mild French mustard.

powder finely ground white (yellow) mustard seeds.

seeded also known as wholegrain. A French-style coarse-grain mustard made from crushed mustard seeds and Dijon-style French mustard.

NOODLES

fresh rice thick, wide, almost white in colour; made from rice and vegetable oil. Must be covered with boiling water to remove starch and excess oil before using in soups and stir-fries.

hokkien also known as stir-fry noodles; fresh egg noodles resembling thick, yellow-brown spaghetti needing no pre-cooking before being used.

rice stick a dried noodle, available flat and wide or very thin; made from rice flour and water.

ONIONS

brown and white are interchangeable. Their pungent flesh adds flavour to a vast range of dishes.

green also known as scallion or (incorrectly) shallot; an immature onion picked before the bulb has formed, having a long, bright-green edible stalk.

red also known as Spanish, red Spanish or Bermuda onion; a sweet-flavoured, large, purple-red onion that is particularly good eaten in raw salads.

PARSLEY, FLAT-LEAF also known as continental parsley or italian parsley.

PATTY-PAN SQUASH very small, young squash also known as summer squash or scaloppine. Yellow or green thin-skinned squash.

PIDE also known as Turkish bread; comes in long (about 45cm) flat loaves as well as individual rounds; made from wheat flour and sprinkled with sesame or black onion seeds.

PITTA (Lebanese bread) also spelled pita; this wheat-flour pocket bread is sold in large, flat pieces that separate easily into two thin rounds. Also available in small thick pieces called pocket pitta.

POLENTA a flour-like cereal made of ground corn (maize); coarse-textured cornmeal. Also the name of the dish made from it

PORK

fillet skinless, boneless eye-fillet cut from the loin.

mince also known as ground pork

steak also known as schnitzel; thin slices usually cut from the leg or rump.

RAISINS large, dark brown dried sweet grapes.

RHUBARB is a vegetable related to sorrel and only the firm, reddish stems are eaten. It's normally sweetened and eaten as a dessert.

RICE

arborio small, round-grain rice well-suited to absorb a large amount of liquid; especially suitable for risotto.

basmati a white fragrant long-grain rice.

brown natural whole-grain.

calrose medium-grain; can be used instead of both long- and short-grain varieties.

jasmine fragrant long-grain rice; white rice can be substituted but will not taste the same.

long-grain elongated-grain, remains separate when cooked; most popular steaming rice in Asia.

wild blackish brown seed from North America is not a member of the rice family. Expensive because of the difficulty in cultivating; has a delicious nutty flavour.

RICE PAPER SHEETS mostly from Vietnam (banh trang). Made from rice paste and stamped into rounds, with a woven pattern. Stores well at room temperature, although they are quite brittle and will break if dropped. Dipped momentarily in water they become pliable wrappers for fried food and for eating fresh (uncooked) vegetables.

RISONI small rice-shaped pasta; similar to orzo and puntalette.

SAFFRON made from the stigma of a particular kind of crocus, saffron is available in strands or ground; imparts a yellow-orange colour and distinctive taste when used in cooking.

SAUCES

fish also called nam pla or nuoc nam; made from pulverised salted fermented fish, most often anchovies. Has a pungent smell and strong taste; use sparingly

hoisin a thick, sweet and spicy Chinese paste made from salted fermented soy beans, onions and garlic; used as a marinade or baste, or to accent stir-fries and barbecued or roasted foods.

ketjap manis Indonesian sweet, thick soy sauce which has sugar and spices added.

oyster Asian in origin, this rich, brown sauce is made from oysters and their brine, cooked with salt and soy sauce, and thickened with starches.

sweet chilli a comparatively mild, Thai-type sauce made from red chillies, sugar, garlic and vinegar.

SESAME

seeds black and white are the most common of the oval seeds harvested from the tropical plant *Sesamum indicum* ; however there are red and brown varieties also. Used in za'atar, halva and tahini and a good source of calcium. To toast, spread seeds evenly on oven tray; toast in moderate oven briefly.

oil made from roasted, crushed, white sesame seeds; a flavouring rather than a cooking medium.

SNOW PEAS also called mange tout ("eat all").

SOY SAUCE made from fermented soy beans. Several variations are available in most supermarkets and Asian food stores.

dark used for colour as well as flavour, particularly in North Chinese cooking.

light as the name suggests, it is light in colour and not as salty as the Chinese variety. We used a light soy sauce of Japanese origin.

salt-reduced we used a sauce with 46% of the salt removed after it is made.

SUGAR we used coarse granulated table sugar, also known as crystal sugar, unless otherwise specified.

brown a soft, fine sugar retaining molasses.

caster also known as superfine or finely granulated table sugar.

pure icing sugar also known as confectioners' sugar or powdered sugar.

raw natural brown granulated sugar.

TABASCO brand name of an extremely fiery sauce made from vinegar, hot red peppers and salt.

TOFU also known as bean curd, an off-white, custard-like product made from the milk of crushed soy beans; comes fresh as soft or firm, and processed as fried or pressed dried sheets.

TORTILLA unleavened bread sold frozen, fresh or vacuum-packed; made from wheat flour ("fajita tortillas") or corn (maize) meal ("enchilada tortillas").

VINEGAR

balsamic authentic only from the province of Modena, Italy; made from a regional wine of white Trebbiano grapes specially processed then aged in antique wooden casks to give the exquisite pungent flavour.

white made from spirit of cane sugar.

white wine made from white wine.

WATER CHESTNUTS resemble chestnuts in appearance but are small brown tubers with a crisp, white, nutty-tasting flesh. Best used fresh, however, canned water chestnuts are more easily obtained and can be kept, under refrigeration, about a month once opened.

zucchini also known as courgette.

make your own stock

These recipes can be made up to 4 days ahead and stored, covered, in the refrigerator. Be sure to remove any fat from the surface after the cooled stock has been refrigerated overnight. If the stock is to be kept longer, it is best to freeze it in smaller quantities. *All stock recipes make about 2.5 litres (10 cups).*

Stock is also available in cans or tetra packs. Stock cubes or powder can be used. As a guide, 1 teaspoon of stock powder or 1 small crumbled stock cube mixed with 1 cup (250ml) water will give a fairly strong stock. Be aware of the salt and fat content of stock cubes and powders and prepared stocks.

BEEF STOCK

2kg meaty beef bones
2 medium onions (300g)
2 sticks celery, chopped
2 medium carrots (250g), chopped
3 bay leaves
2 teaspoons black peppercorns
5 litres (20 cups) water
3 litres (12 cups) water, extra

Place bones and unpeeled chopped onions in baking dish. Bake in hot oven about 1 hour or until bones and onions are well browned. Transfer bones and onions to large pan, add celery, carrots, bay leaves, peppercorns and water, simmer, uncovered, 3 hours. Add extra water, simmer, uncovered, further 1 hour; strain.

CHICKEN STOCK

2kg chicken bones
2 medium onions (300g), chopped
2 sticks celery, chopped
2 medium carrots (250g), chopped
3 bay leaves
2 teaspoons black peppercorns
5 litres (20 cups) water

Combine ingredients in large pan, simmer, uncovered, 2 hours; strain.

FISH STOCK

1.5kg fish bones
3 litres (12 cups) water
1 medium onion (150g), chopped
2 sticks celery, chopped
2 bay leaves
1 teaspoon black peppercorns

Combine ingredients in large pan, simmer, uncovered, 20 minutes; strain.

VEGETABLE STOCK

2 large carrots (360g), chopped
2 large parsnips (360g), chopped
4 medium onions (600g), chopped
12 sticks celery, chopped
4 bay leaves
2 teaspoons black peppercorns
6 litres (24 cups) water

Combine ingredients in large pan, simmer, uncovered, 1½ hours; strain.

facts and figures

Wherever you live, you'll be able to use our recipes with the help of these easy-to-follow conversions. While these conversions are approximate only, the difference between an exact and the approximate conversion of various liquid and dry measures is but minimal and will not affect your cooking results.

dry measures

metric	imperial
15g	1/2oz
30g	1oz
60g	2oz
90g	3oz
125g	4oz (1/4lb)
155g	5oz
185g	6oz
220g	7oz
250g	8oz (1/2lb)
280g	9oz
315g	10oz
345g	11oz
375g	12oz (3/4lb)
410g	13oz
440g	14oz
470g	15oz
500g	16oz (1lb)
750g	24oz (11/2lb)
1kg	32oz (2lb)

liquid measures

metric	imperial
30ml	1 fluid oz
60ml	2 fluid oz
100ml	3 fluid oz
125ml	4 fluid oz
150ml	5 fluid oz (1/4 pint/1 gill)
190ml	6 fluid oz
250ml	8 fluid oz
300ml	10 fluid oz (1/2 pint)
500ml	16 fluid oz
600ml	20 fluid oz (1 pint)
1000ml (1 litre)	13/4 pints

helpful measures

metric	imperial
3mm	1/8in
6mm	1/4in
1cm	1/2in
2cm	3/4in
2.5cm	1in
5cm	2in
6cm	21/2in
8cm	3in
10cm	4in
13cm	5in
15cm	6in
18cm	7in
20cm	8in
23cm	9in
25cm	10in
28cm	11in
30cm	12in (1ft)

helpful measures

The difference between one country's measuring cups and another's is, at most, within a 2 or 3 teaspoon variance. (For the record, 1 Australian metric measuring cup holds approximately 250ml.) The most accurate way of measuring dry ingredients is to weigh them. When measuring liquids, use a clear glass or plastic jug with the metric markings. (One Australian metric tablespoon holds 20ml; one Australian metric teaspoon holds 5ml.)

If you would like to purchase *The Australian Women's Weekly* Test Kitchen's metric measuring cups and spoons (as approved by Standards Australia), turn to page 120 for details and order coupon. You will receive:

- a graduated set of 4 cups for measuring dry ingredients, with sizes marked on the cups.
- a graduated set of 4 spoons for measuring dry and liquid ingredients, with amounts marked on the spoons.

Note: North America, NZ and the UK use 15ml tablespoons. All cup and spoon measurements are level.

We use large eggs having an average weight of 60g.

oven temperatures

These oven temperatures are only a guide. Always check the manufacturer's manual.

	°C (Celsius)	°F (Fahrenheit)	Gas Mark
Very slow	120	250	1
Slow	150	300	2
Moderately slow	160	325	3
Moderate	180 - 190	350 - 375	4
Moderately hot	200 - 210	400 - 425	5
Hot	220 - 230	450 - 475	6
Very hot	240 - 250	500 - 525	7

how to measure

When using graduated metric measuring cups, shake dry ingredients loosely into the appropriate cup. Do not tap the cup on a bench or tightly pack the ingredients unless directed to do so. Level top of measuring cups and measuring spoons with a knife. When measuring liquids, place a clear glass or plastic jug with metric markings on a flat surface to check accuracy at eye level.

Looking after **your interest...**

Keep your ACP cookbooks clean, tidy and within easy reach with slipcovers designed to hold up to 12 books. *Plus* you can follow our recipes perfectly with a set of accurate measuring cups and spoons, as used by *The Australian Women's Weekly* Test Kitchen.

To order

Mail or fax Photocopy and complete the coupon below and post to ACP Books Reader Offer, ACP Publishing, GPO Box 4967, Sydney NSW 2001, or fax to (02) 9267 4967.

Phone Have your credit card details ready, then phone 136 116 (Mon-Fri, 8.00am-6.00pm; Sat, 8.00am-6.00pm).

Price

Book Holder
Australia: $13.10 (incl. GST).
Elsewhere: $A21.95.

Metric Measuring Set
Australia: $6.50 (incl. GST).
New Zealand: $A8.00.
Elsewhere: $A9.95.
Prices include postage and handling.
This offer is available in all countries.

Payment

Australian residents We accept the credit cards listed on the coupon, money orders and cheques.

Overseas residents We accept the credit cards listed on the coupon, drafts in $A drawn on an Australian bank, and also British, New Zealand and U.S. cheques in the currency of the country of issue. Credit card charges are at the exchange rate current at the time of payment.

Photocopy and complete the coupon below

☐ **Book Holder**

☐ **Metric Measuring Set**
Please indicate number(s) required.

Mr/Mrs/Ms _____

Address _____

_____

Postcode _____ Country _____

Ph: Bus. Hours:( ) _____

I enclose my cheque/money order for $ _____
payable to ACP Publishing

OR: please charge my

☐ Bankcard ☐ Visa ☐ MasterCard

☐ Diners Club ☐ Amex

Card number

Expiry date ____/____

Cardholder's signature _____

Please allow up to 30 days for delivery within Australia.
Allow up to 6 weeks for overseas deliveries.
Both offers expire 31/12/02. HLLFF02

Designer *Hieu Nguyen*
Sub-editor *Deborah Quick*
Test Kitchen Staff
Food director *Pamela Clark*
Food editor *Karen Hammial*
Assistant food editor *Amira Ibram*
Test kitchen manager *Elizabeth Hooper*
Senior home economist *Kimberley Coverdale*
Home economists *Emma Braz,*
Kelly Cruickshanks, Sarah Hine, Sarah Hobbs,
Naomi Scesny, Alison Webb
ACP Books Staff
Editorial director *Susan Tomnay*
Creative director *Hieu Nguyen*
Senior writer and editor *Georgina Bitcon*
Senior editor *Liz Neate*
Chief sub-editor *Julie Collard*
Sub-editor *Deborah Quick*
Designers *Mary Keep, Ayesha Ali Raza,*
Caryl Wiggins, Alison Windmill
Studio manager *Caryl Wiggins*
Editorial coordinator *Holly van Oyen*
Editorial assistant *Georgie McShane*
Publishing manager (sales) *Jennifer McDonald*
Publishing manager (rights & new projects)
Jane Hazell
Production manager *Carol Currie*
Business manager *Sally Lees*
Chief executive officer *John Alexander*
Group publisher *Jill Baker*
Publisher *Sue Wannan*

Produced by ACP Books, Sydney.
Colour separations by ACP Colour
Graphics Pty Ltd, Sydney.
Printed by Dai Nippon Printing in Korea.
Published by ACP Publishing Pty Limited,
54 Park St, Sydney; GPO Box 4088,
Sydney, NSW 1028.
Ph: (02) 9282 8618 Fax: (02) 9267 9438.
To order books, phone 136 116.
acpbooks@acp.com.au
www.acpbooks.com.au
AUSTRALIA: Distributed by Network
Distribution Company, GPO Box 4088,
Sydney, NSW 1028. Ph: (02) 9282 8777
Fax: (02) 9264 3278.
UNITED KINGDOM: Distributed by Australian
Consolidated Press (UK), Moulton Park
Business Centre, Red House Rd, Moulton Park,
Northampton, NN3 6AQ Ph: (01604) 497 531
Fax: (01604) 497 533 acpukltd@aol.com
CANADA: Distributed by Whitecap Books Ltd,
351 Lynn Ave, North Vancouver, BC, V7J 2C4,
Ph: (604) 980 9852.
NEW ZEALAND: Distributed by Netlink
Distribution Company, Level 4, 23 Hargreaves St,
College Hill, Auckland 1, Ph: (9) 302 7616.
SOUTH AFRICA: Distributed by PSD Promotions
(Pty) Ltd, PO Box 1175, Isando 1600, SA,
Ph: (011) 392 6065,
and CNA Limited, Newsstand Division,
PO Box 10799, Johannesburg 2000, SA,
Ph: (011) 491 7500.

Simplylite low-fat feasts
Includes index.
ISBN 1 86396 259 X
1. Low-fat diet – Recipes. 2. Cookery.
(Series: Australian Women's Weekly).
641.5638